MW00478526

Terrence Malick |

Contemporary Film Directors

Edited by James Naremore

The Contemporary Film Directors series provides concise, well-written introductions to directors from around the world and from every level of the film industry. Its chief aims are to broaden our awareness of important artists, to give serious critical attention to their work, and to illustrate the variety and vitality of contemporary cinema. Contributors to the series include an array of internationally respected critics and academics. Each volume contains an incisive critical commentary, an informative interview with the director, and a detailed filmography.

A list of books in the series appears at the end of this book.

Terrence Malick |

Lloyd Michaels

UNIVERSITY
OF
ILLINOIS
PRESS
URBANA
AND
CHICAGO

∞ This book is printed on acid-free paper.

Library of Congress Cataloging-in-Publication Data
Michaels, Lloyd.
Terrence Malick / Lloyd Michaels.
p. cm. — (Contemporary film directors)
Includes bibliographical references and index.
ISBN 978-0-252-03385-8 (cl : alk. paper)
ISBN 978-0-252-07575-9 (pbk : alk. paper)
1. Malick, Terrence, 1945– I. Title.
PN1998.3.M3388M53   2009
791.43023'3092—dc22 [B]   2008012689

For Mary and Jack

Contents |

My interest in Terrence Malick dates back to his first two features, which immediately found their way into my introductory film survey, then titled Film as Narrative Art. *Badlands* and *Days of Heaven* were obvious choices in the late 1970s, as their formal beauty, carefully crafted screenplays, and existentialist themes applied the traditions of the European art cinema to essential American myths. While this course evolved over the years and incorporated more experimental as well as mainstream films, one or the other of Malick's idiosyncratic diptych nearly always made the syllabus—if only to keep the director's name alive.

With the surprising announcement in 1998 of Malick's return after several rumored false starts, the first book-length studies—James Morrison and Thomas Schur's *The Films of Terrence Malick* and Hannah Patterson's anthology *The Cinema of Terrence Malick: Poetic Visions of America,* along with Michel Chion's monograph for the British Film Institute on *The Thin Red Line*—confirmed the significance of an auteur who could now be said to have created a genuine oeuvre. The book I have written becomes the first to consider all four of Malick's films to date. In addition to offering a comprehensive introduction to his work, I hope it may stimulate a reconsideration of *The New World,* which has so far suffered from scholarly neglect.

In accordance with the previous volumes in the Contemporary Directors series, I have sought to describe the trajectory of Malick's creative development while employing close analysis of some paradigmatic moments in each of his films. I suggest that the most recent works represent a discernible shift from philosophical to religious concerns and relate certain major themes in his work—migration and the open road, violence and war, the sublime in nature, the restless yearning of the human heart—to classic texts in American literature. The biographical portions remain necessarily sketchy, given the director's notorious insistence on privacy. No secrets of Malick's personal life or filmmaking practices will be herein revealed. If this book can lay claim to originality, it lies in the literary sensibility I frequently apply to Malick's cinema. This approach is partly a product of my academic training and partly a reflection of what I take to be the director's own sensibility. Malick and I are near contemporaries, similarly educated at New England universities. The critical premises from which I study his work—subordinating intentionality and ideology to issues of thematic development and aesthetic design—seem consistent with Malick's apparent artistic ideals. I have tried to enrich my formalist and humanist tendencies with a careful consideration of cultural history and intertextual references, all in the belief that the best criticism begins with appreciation and wonder, proceeds with engagement and attentiveness, and ends with a paradoxical blend of conviction and openness.

| | |

I am grateful to Allegheny College for providing a sabbatical leave during which the manuscript was written and to the college's Academic Support Committee for a grant to support my research. Thanks to my colleague, Laura Reeck, for translating Michel Ciment's important interview with Malick, and to Walter Metz, who scrupulously read my final draft and offered several suggestions that found their (uncredited) way into the text. Alla Meleshevich displayed remarkable patience along with technical expertise in helping me to prepare the illustrations. Walter Metz and Arthur Nolletti Jr. provided excellent commentaries on my manuscript; Art, in particular, has been an inspiring colleague and wonderful friend throughout my professional life. The series editor, James Naremore, whose own scholarship drew me to propose writing this book, and Joan Catapano at the University of Illinois Press were supportive partners in bringing the manuscript to publication.

This book is dedicated to my wife, Mary, whom I took on a first date to the movies (*The Organizer*) forty years ago, and to Jack, my dear son.

Terrence Malick |

Terrence Malick: A Cinema in Front of Our Eyes

Is there another American artist—let alone an American filmmaker—who has so regularly been granted genius status after creating such a discontinuous and limited body of work? One who has managed to be revered without ever being popular, admired while remaining essentially unknown? Among writers, Thomas Pynchon comes to mind, but his literary output, while clearly not prolific, has remained relatively steady. Stanley Kubrick, the director most often cited in articles about Terrence Malick's career and cinematic vision, seems positively prolific and transparent by comparison. Malick's achievement in his four films to date seems without precedent, just as the trajectory of his life as a filmmaker—writer, director, and producer—appears unique.

The erratic pattern of his directorial output—four movies in thirty-five years, with a twenty-year hiatus between his second and third films—combined with his early academic training in philosophy and reputation for intellectual brilliance and reclusiveness have set Malick apart from the celebrated generation of young American directors who emerged in the late 1960s and early 1970s, including Arthur Penn, Francis Ford Coppola, Martin Scorsese, Bob Rafelson, Brian DePalma, George Lucas, and Steven Spielberg. Despite belonging to this accomplished group of contemporaries, he has frequently been described (again like Kubrick) as an essentially European filmmaker, with a narrative pace, visual style, and thematic opaqueness more akin to the continental art cinema than the New Hollywood. Readers looking for revelations about "the Runaway Genius" will be better served by Peter Biskind's eponymous article in *Vanity Fair* than by my introduction to the art of Malick's cinema. Instead, as the first study to incorporate all four of his features, this work will try to define certain recurrent concerns and habitual practices that mark his production to date. In keeping with the director's own educational and cultural background, my critical approach will be largely formalist, treating Malick as an American auteur and concentrating on his work as aesthetic objects of contemplation.

The long-anticipated appearance of *The Thin Red Line* (1998) and *The New World* (2005) confirmed Malick's original filmmaking gifts as well as his artistic "integrity," understood as a reluctance to compromise his vision to accommodate the simpler tastes of a new generation of multiplex audiences or the practical suggestions of his crew and an adamant refusal to promote or explain his work. "Malick would never let anyone do anything that went against his own ideas," the great cinematographer Nestor Almendros has reported (237). Despite his absence from premieres, festivals, and even the supplemental materials that now sell many DVDs, both films advertised the maverick "Malick" brand rather than their featured performers (an all-star cast in *The Thin Red Line*) or stories (the Pocahontas myth in *The New World*). As a marketing strategy, an updated version of what Timothy Corrigan has labeled "the commerce of auteurism," this appeal to curiosity about the director was probably doomed to fail. Few regular moviegoers remembered or ever heard of Terrence Malick, and those who did were as likely as not to ignore his resurrection. In any case, like *Badlands* (1973) and *Days of Heaven* (1978), neither "comeback" film met box-office expectations. The critical reviews, while respectful, were rarely enthusiastic. For many cinephiles and professional critics alike, it seemed that Malick's time had passed.

If there is an anachronistic quality to these two most recent films, it may be their avoidance of special effects and computer-generated imagery, on the one hand, and their insistence on visual and auditory spectacle, on the other hand. Malick's movies stubbornly remain a theatrical medium, intended for magnified projection with multichannel sound. With their languorous narrative pace, arresting visual design, simple story lines, and relative paucity of dialogue, they do not comport well with the viewing habits of most Blockbuster patrons; instead, commentators regularly link each of Malick's four films with the aesthetics of the silent cinema. Hwanhee Lee, for example, foregrounds their appeal to "awe and wonder before any impulse to understand and interpret" their meaning. For all their visual attractions, however, Malick's features always aspire to go beyond the visceral effects of his New Hollywood contemporaries. His remains a cerebral cinema at the same time as it approaches, visually and aurally, the sublime.

Thematically as well as stylistically, *The Thin Red Line* and *The New World* contribute to a sense of coherent and continuous activity despite the prolonged interruption that marks Malick's career. Although it is difficult to interpret any single work as expressing his own philosophical or ideological perspective, the last two films do seem to clarify his ongoing thematic preoccupations (most obviously, the grandeur and indifference of nature) and consistent directorial techniques (most obviously, pervasive voiceover). In addition to defining a unified body of work—an oeuvre—*The Thin Red Line* and *The New World* suggest a personal dimension to Malick's filmmaking that is less evident in his first two films. Epic in scope, they nevertheless center on a crisis of individual ambition, a theme only briefly glimpsed in *Badlands* and *Days of Heaven*. In Lieutenant Colonel Tall (Nick Nolte) and especially Captain Smith (Colin Farrell), Malick creates two talented, alienated leaders whose accomplishments in service to a national mission come at the price of lost years of fruitless striving. In the 1970s, he had portrayed Kit (Martin Sheen) in *Badlands* and Bill (Richard Gere) in *Days of Heaven* with a detachment less strongly felt in the later films. For the first time, one senses the director's identification with his most recent protagonist, Captain John Smith, whose quest for glorious discoveries results in professional disappointment as his boundless projects go unfinanced and personal isolation as he travels a narrow path alone.

The Thin Red Line and *The New World* also depict more directly than the 1970s films Malick's interest in certain national myths as they shape the destinies of his major characters. Rather than being defined in psychological terms, his protagonists are all to some degree products of economic and cultural forces that they are powerless to control and that they imperfectly comprehend, but the particular historical circumstances of World War II and the founding of the Jamestown colony play a more prominent role in shaping the more recent narratives. *Days of Heaven* takes place within a discernible time and place in American history, but, as its title suggests, its mythic dimensions are more biblical than national. Although ostensibly situated in the Texas Panhandle (shot in Alberta), its landscape evokes the Fertile Crescent and Eden rather than any particular location in the American Southwest. *The New World* also conjures images of Eden—indeed, each of Malick's films incorporates its own fragile Paradise—but never loses touch with its specific setting, the Virginia settlement at Jamestown (where the film was actually shot), framing the epic narrative with dissolves of historical maps of the region in the opening and closing credits. As the Badlands and the wheat ranch are largely symbolic landscapes, Kit and Bill remain character types, influenced by images and values of American popular culture: Kit tries to give shape to his dissociated personality by imitating James Dean, the rebel without a cause; Bill is seduced and betrayed by capitalism's promise of "the big score." Still, their alienation and criminality are constructed as universal issues, derived at least as much from Albert Camus and Emile Zola as from Nicholas Ray or John Steinbeck. In *The Thin Red Line* and especially *The New World,* the fate of the American nation more firmly asserts priority over the fate of individuals.

Perhaps the most consistent quality among Malick's four features to date has been their resistance to the irony, fragmentation, and lack of conviction that characterizes postmodernism as well as much of modern cinema. Instead, to apply terms from literary history rather than the more customary philosophical labels that have been attached to his work, Malick seems a stubbornly romantic artist in depicting the isolated individual's desire for transcendence amidst established social institutions, the grandeur and untouched beauty of nature, the competing claims of instinct and reason, and the lure of the open road. He is no less a naturalist, however, in his portrayal of the indifference of nature and the determinism that rules man's fate. James Morrison and Thomas Schur have described this paradoxical aspect of Malick's art as an attempt, following Martin Heidegger, to redefine transcendence as quotidian experience (100). When looking for influences on his sensibility—and everyone has—one might as well call on Ralph Waldo Emerson and Walt Whitman as Heidegger. Malick's filmmaking is often called visionary or poetic, which John Orr identifies as recording a "sacred immediacy, in which advanced technologies have recovered the possibility of the sacred in a secular world" ("Cinema" 135). This impulse takes us back to American transcendentalism and Emerson's ecstatic vision of becoming a "transparent eyeball" in the midst of the Concord woods, to which Malick adds Emily Dickinson's melancholy awareness that "Perception of an Object costs / Precise the Object's loss—" (No. 1071). In contrast to modernism's paradigmatic wasteland or postmodernism's simulacrum, Malick's cinema "restores the beauty and power of the image as a carrier of meaning" (Mottram 14). That meaning may appear persistently undecipherable or unrecoverable, but the camera's fixed attention to the sheer gorgeousness or isolated perfection of the imagery it records insists on a resilient significance as it commands in the audience an irresistible awe. To return to the language of American literary romanticism, like the opening chapter of Herman Melville's *Moby Dick,* Malick's films demand, "Surely all this is not without meaning."

Absent either an authoritative narrator among their many voiceovers or the testimony of the auteur himself, and given their sporadic production and the absence of a critical consensus about their value, these four films require viewers to see and think without external interventions. Perhaps this is their "philosophical" quality. Malick's coterie audience and the opacity of his style have led some critics to regard him as an elitist, but Stanley Cavell's description of modern art gets closer to the truth about his former student's achievement to date: "While the community of serious art is small, it is not exclusive. It is esoteric, but the secret is open to anyone" (14). By eschewing such technical means as rapid editing and special effects, Malick restores the spectator's sense, in Cavell's terms, that everything is "in front of [our] eyes" (xxii), awaiting our making sense of the experience. Such is the project of this little book.

Marks of the Auteur

With four features now completed, Malick has at least created a critical mass sufficient to consider their common attributes as constituting a sustained artistic vision. Because he has written as well as directed each of his screenplays, we may justifiably identify him as the author of his films. But if Malick's cinema lends itself to auteurist analysis, he remains a filmmaker almost without precedent or influence. While younger filmmakers like Harmony Korine, Christopher Munch, and David Gordon Green have been cited as acolytes and Oliver Stone's *Natural Born Killers* (1994) described as an homage to *Badlands,* Malick's own work stands apart (Morrison and Schur 30–31). Like Yasujiro Ozu, Robert Bresson, and Eric Rohmer, he has produced a genre unto himself, one best described simply by applying his name. His signature can be discerned in several recurrent concerns beyond the two formal qualities of his work already mentioned: the grandiose representation of nature and the distinctive employment of subjective voiceover narration.

Whatever their ultimate evaluation of the quality of a particular work, reviewers have repeatedly acknowledged Malick's ambition and assurance. The director whose cinema may most closely parallel Malick's own is his near contemporary, Werner Herzog. Especially Herzog's earlier films—*Signs of Life, Fata Morgana, Aguirre, Wrath of God,* and *Hearts of Glass*—reverberate with the same audacious drive to "'get images nobody had ever seen before,'" which a colleague described as Malick's obsessive motivation (qtd. in Biskind, "Runaway" 204). Herzog also shares Malick's epic impulse, along with his tendency to employ remarkable musical sound tracks and to depict alienated, primitive, or dissociated characters without resorting to psychological explanations for their behavior.

Like Herzog, Malick makes movies about history but also about the time of their own production. *Badlands,* for example, is set in the 1950s and based on real-life characters and events, the killing spree of Charles Starkweather and Caril Ann Fugate, but the protagonists more clearly reflect Arthur Penn's version of Clyde Barrow and Bonnie Parker than their actual progenitors. Similarly, *The Thin Red Line,* while ostensibly depicting the American assault on Guadalcanal, hardly names its specific geographical location and, as John Hodgkins suggests, reflects the ideology of the first Persian Gulf War rather than the Second World War. Malick's retreat from postmodernism, it seems, involves eliding the course of history with a meditation on universal conflict and change.

Another index of this interest in the universal aspect of human experience can be found in Malick's construction of character. His protagonists, even when they are recognizable historical personages, like Kit (Starkweather) or Captain Smith, deliberately lack psychological depth, so much so that they are often barely recognizable as individuals. It is possible, for example, to watch *Days of Heaven* without being aware of a single character's proper name. Because the actors cast as enlisted men physically resemble one another, rarely converse, and are usually seen in full uniform, it can be difficult to distinguish the individual soldiers in *The Thin Red Line,* while in *The New World,* one of the three major characters, John Rolfe, is never identified by name. In both later films, the heavily accented or overlapping dialogue and multiple nondiegetic voices further blur the recognition of individual personalities.

By deliberately creating flat characters without background or other personal traits, Malick imposes a distanciation that requires the audience to engage with a film's (increasingly metaphysical) ideas or to view human figures as part of a larger design instead of identifying with the dramatic conflicts of its characters. His oppositional pairs, like Bill and the Farmer, Witt and Welsh, Smith and Rolfe, thus may "appear as objects and function metaphorically" (Morrison and Schur 94) without fully involving our sympathies. Unable to recognize the heroes of character-driven classical Hollywood narratives, Malick's audience may be uncertain how to characterize these figures, cautiously responding to his protagonists with platitudes like the deputy's, "You're quite an individual, Kit," at the conclusion of *Badlands,* and wondering about the manacled prisoner's final cryptic expression: "Think they'll take that into consideration?" However seriously we may regard these characters or consider their behavior, they remain set apart from us, viewed almost exclusively in long shot and understood as representatives rather than idiosyncratic human beings with an existence beyond the diegesis.

Beginning with Kit, Malick has created a series of major characters—Bill and the Farmer, Witt, Pocahontas—all of whom die young, yet with a placidity that belies their doomed fate. Kit responds to the deputy's concluding compliment with a self-satisfied grin as Holly (Sissy Spacek) describes his execution in flat voiceover; Bill's flight from the armed posse ends with a startling cut to a silent, slow-motion, underwater view of his final moment in the shallow waters, followed by a long shot of the dead man's float. What was probably perceived as a measure of Kit's pathology and was conveyed through technique in *Days of Heaven* becomes in the last two films a more self-conscious evocation of something spiritual and self-fulfilling, approximating grace. In contrast to the grisly, absurd death of Sergeant Keck earlier in *The Thin Red Line*, Witt faces his execution at the hands of the Japanese with a transcendence that fulfills his yearning to die with the same tranquility as his mother. Pocahontas's premature passing takes place off-camera, unexpectedly, following her self-composed final meeting with Smith and calm return to her family. "Mother," she says before falling fatally ill, "now I know where you live." Although her fate may seem tragic given the strange turns her life has taken, Malick confirms her Native American spirituality by avoiding a deathbed scene and denying the audience its attendant catharsis.

The poignancy of Pocahontas's unanticipated, unseen death derives from her dislocation in the court of King James as well as her reunion with Smith in the formal gardens surrounding the palace. Although the transformed Indian princess, now Mrs. Rebecca Rolfe, appears tranquil in her London surroundings, the ornate scenery serves to remind viewers of the native paradise she has left behind. No less than Witt, whom we see AWOL on a tropical island in the Pacific in the opening sequence of *The Thin Red Line*, she has been exiled from Eden, having perceived only a fleeting sense of personal wholeness and natural harmony. Both characters reflect Malick's "vision of the world as paradise and paradise lost, caught up in darkness and death but open to redemption through the radiance of unselfish individual action" (Silberman 171). The less "radiant" protagonists of the first two films are allowed their moment of communion with nature as well, but without redemptive self-sacrifice. Thus, the three runaways in *Days of Heaven* experience but a single season of bliss before their fragile happiness is splintered by passion, plague, and war, while Kit and Holly manage a peaceful, if even briefer sojourn deep in the forest before civilization in the form of a sheriff's posse—"bounty hunters," Kit calls them—drives them from their one experience of tranquility, if not transcendence. Each of these Edenic episodes, in retrospect, expresses Malick's romantic ideal of human oneness with nature, along with the equally romantic sense that such moments cannot possibly be sustained.

In contrast to Pocahontas's concordance with her changing environment, Malick's male protagonists, beginning most clearly with Kit and Bill but also including Smith and Witt, remain fundamentally alienated in their uneasy if not simply hostile relationship with civilization. While Kit pauses to appreciate a few passing sights during his flight from the law—he advises Holly to quit "bitching" and "enjoy the scenery"—and pays lip service to respecting the majority view when he speaks into a Dictaphone, he remains, to the end, a sociopath. Bill's equally marginalized social status provokes a murderous rage against his bosses, first the foreman, then the Farmer. Early in *The Thin Red Line,* Private Witt returns to Charlie Company in the brig, engaged in defiant dialogue with Sergeant Welsh; similarly, Smith is first seen arriving in the New World in chains, a prisoner of Captain Newport for acts of insubordination. Compared to the superficiality of Kit's and Bill's touristy contentment, the two soldiers' idyllic relationship with the natural world makes them seem almost like noble savages, but all four men ultimately fail to manage successfully the social contract. Their alienation from society's institutions may reflect Malick's own uneasy negotiations with the "establishment," be that understood as academia, Hollywood, or perhaps even America itself. But the director has remained, like his characters, ultimately too distant for us to judge, and the foregoing suggestion amounts to no more than speculation.

In addition to these repeated thematic parallels, Malick's recurrent stylistic choices, which will be analyzed in greater detail as they occur in specific works, constitute a distinctive cinematic signature. He prefers to shoot outdoors using natural light. Almendros, who won an Academy Award for the cinematography in *Days of Heaven,* has described how the director particularly favors "the magic hour," the last moments of available daylight after sunset, for its dramatic effect. "For these few minutes the light is truly magical, because no one knows where it is coming from. The sun is not to be seen, but the sky can be bright. And the blue of the atmosphere undergoes strange mutations. Malick's intuition and daring probably made these scenes the most interesting ones visually in the film" (243). Critics have disagreed over the efficacy of the director's exceptional visual sensibility. Even Almendros suggests that some rushes for *Days of Heaven* were "brilliantly executed, but with too much virtuosity" (240). This suspicion about the films' painterly qualities has persisted. Gilbert Adair, for example, denounces *The Thin Red Line* for being "'bludgeoned by gorgeousness'" (qtd. in McCann 80). Ron Mottram's spirited defense of the director's lush mise-en-scène, however, describes an essentially conservative aesthetic: "In a period in the history of the visual arts in which the image is often sacrificed to a shallow conceptualism, he restores the beauty and power of the image as a carrier of meaning" (13–14).

Malick's beautiful compositions on screen generally take one of two forms: panoramic vistas of the natural landscape, often employing a telephoto lens and a smoothly moving camera, or carefully arranged static close-ups of exotic objects held long enough to become cinematic still lifes. Human beings may be either entirely absent from these images (the pair of wine glasses and decanter on the side table in *Days of Heaven*; the coconut sprout on the beach at the end of *The Thin Red Line*), or they may appear as props in the mise-en-scène (Kit with rifle slung across his back gazing at the horizon in *Badlands*; the natives stalking Smith in the forest in *The New World*). The effect is much the same, expressing "the autonomous beauty of things" (Orr, "Cinema," 134) and, in a manner similar to Malick's use of voiceover, contrasting with the insipidness, harshness, or violence of the action, creating a kind of counterpoint.

In documentary, memoir, and film noir, voiceover narration generally serves an explanatory function that often produces a scripted quality to speech. Only Holly's recounting of events in *Badlands* seems scripted, however, its banality never rising to the level of explanation. Linda's narration in *Days of Heaven*, although hardly revelatory, conveys a spontaneity and sensitivity entirely lacking in Holly's speech. With the multiple voiceovers in *The Thin Red Line* and *The New World*, "the meditative dimensions of unspoken inner speech" (Sterritt 13) completely supersede any narrative function. Malick's enduring interest in voiceover now seems evident: he cares for the sheer sound of the human voice as well as its suggestiveness, just as his visual compositions convey an autonomous beauty and luminous expressiveness as they stand apart from the immediacy of the drama. Linda's musings on apocalypse ("I met a guy named Ding Dong") may seem more appealing because they amount to an untutored vernacular poetry, but Witt and Pocahontas employ a more exalted language in pursuit of the same evanescent understanding of life's ultimate mystery.

"A Blossom Fell"

The signature elements that comprise a "Malick film" crystallize for the first time in a self-contained scene near the end of *Badlands*, the "dance in the headlights" to Nat King Cole's beautiful ballad, "A Blossom Fell." Kit drives the runaway couple's stolen Cadillac across the prairie towards the Canadian border and the dream of escape, somewhere in the darkness between "the gas fires of Missoula and the lights of Cheyenne." Holly has already told us that the romance is over for her, but Kit's hopes revive as he views the distant mountains and imagines a new identity for himself as a Canadian Mountie. The isolation and wonder of the moment bring Holly to an epiphany: "I felt all kinds of things looking at the lights of Cheyenne, but most important, I made up my mind never again to tag along with the hell-bent type no matter how much in love with him I was." Her flat affect and hackneyed expressions immediately refute any fresh insight, however. The characterization of Kit, which repeats the clichéd quality of her earlier description of him as "the most trigger-happy person I'd ever met," now seems pathetic rather than ironic and even funny in its inadequacy. Kit himself is exhausted, compulsively making small talk ("runnin' off at the mouth, as usual") that his girlfriend politely ignores ("I'm sorry, I wasn't listening"). A white bird can be seen in the headlights fluttering away from the approaching car, indifferent to the couple's fate.

Kit is aroused from his lethargy when Holly goes to turn off the radio. "Nat King Cole!" he proclaims, and the volume rises to the strains of the popular song—heard with perfect fidelity despite the remoteness of their location. Malick cuts to total darkness, then the luminous blue of Kit's denim jacket breaks the lower right corner of the frame. Kit and Holly dance close in the light of an undisclosed spotlight, embracing the "radiance," as Witt might call it, as much as each other. Significantly, the camera views them at first in mid-shot from a slightly low angle, expressing the intimacy and apparent glory of the interlude, then subtly rises and pulls back slightly, diminishing their stature as they recede into mid-frame while the lyrics are amplified:

I thought you loved me, you said you loved me,
We planned together to dream forever.
The dream has ended, for true love died,
The night a blossom fell and touched two lips that lied.

Genuinely responsive for perhaps the only time in the film, discarding his James Dean persona and approaching a sense of wholeness and authenticity that is the elusive goal of all of Malick's protagonists, Kit tries to achieve his own epiphany in words hardly more original than Holly's but infinitely more expressive: "Boy, if I could sing a song like that, if I could sing a song about the way I feel right now. . . ." He pauses, searching for the right phrase. "It'd be a hit." For a filmmaker frequently accused of emotional detachment and philosophical abstraction, this is an immensely moving moment, intensified by Martin Sheen's affecting delivery of the line. Kit is no hero, tragic or otherwise, but in this instant he gives sincere voice to his desire to escape his own tough-guy role at the same time that he acknowledges his personal inadequacy to the task.

In another startling cut, Malick reveals the source of the shining light, the Cadillac's beams penetrating the darkness to the right, where the camera pans to find Kit and Holly, now in long shot. The music continues, nondiegetically, when the scene switches to sunrise, the car still traveling towards the mountains as Holly's voiceover returns to tell

us, "Kit knew the end was coming," and the song's sad refrain ("The dream has ended") offers concluding commentary.

This scene resonates beyond its lyrical poignancy because the sense of loss it projects extends to the very process of cinematic signification. Malick has designed the widescreen mise-en-scène—the headlights illuminating the shadowy figures flickering in their beam—to be precisely analogous to the projection occurring in the movie theatre. Moreover, Holly's retrospective narration reminds us of the evanescent, illusory quality of the image itself: she has just announced the end of her romantic feeling for Kit, and viewers may recall her foretelling of Kit's imminent demise in her first voiceover, in which she describes how her story will end "in the Badlands of Montana." The entropy that engulfs this sequence is also analogous to the way most movies, at least in the classical era, seem to wind down, to lose their energy in the course of their mechanical projection. Cavell makes this point eloquently in *The World Viewed*: "The reels on a projector, like the bulbs of an hourglass, repeat something else [than the roundness of clocks]: that as the past fills up, the future thins" (75).

Much of Malick's filmmaking after *Badlands* includes similar sustained moments of self-reflexivity. Here, the configuration of projected light into darkness in the scene's establishing shot (placed at the end), the nondiegetic presences of the absent (and older) Holly as narrator and Nat King Cole, and the entropic aspect of the action all suggest a particular paradigm of cinema: the mechanical apparatus of shooting and projection with its play of presence and absence, its recalling the presentness of the past. Cavell has suggested how "pride of place within the canon of serious films will be found occupied by those films that most clearly and most deeply discover the powers of the medium itself" (219). By this standard, at least, Malick surely belongs in the pantheon of modern directors.

"A Sort of Cinematic Salinger": A Brief Biography of Terrence Malick

This description, comparing the intensely private director to the equally reclusive, less productive writer, appears at the beginning of Peter Biskind's lengthy 1998 portrait in *Vanity Fair*, published on the occasion of Malick's return to the public's attention with the release of *The Thin Red Line*. It seems an apt analogy, considering not only the filmmaker's acknowledged brilliance and long retreat from view but also the personal eccentricities reported in the article. Given his return and subsequent engagement with a variety of film projects, however, including the completion of *The New World*, the Salinger label may no longer apply. Like myself, Biskind, a true Hollywood insider who wrote admiringly of a younger Malick in his gossipy, fascinating book about the New Hollywood, *Easy Riders, Raging Bulls* (1998), was frustrated by his subject's refusal to be interviewed for the magazine article but nevertheless offers probably the most detailed, trustworthy depiction of the mature filmmaker currently available. Like Malick's own protagonists, however, the bearded character who appears in Biskind's pages remains but a phantom, leaving readers with more questions than answers. What does seem clear since his last interviews nearly thirty years ago is that the director wishes for his movies to speak for themselves. That desire will be respected here and will provide the basis for the critical methodology of this study. The outlines of the director's life nonetheless provide some tantalizing insights into his body of work.

This much we know about Terrence Malick. He was born on November 30, 1943, in Ottawa, Illinois, the eldest son of Emil, a geologist of Lebanese descent ("Malick" means "king" in Lebanese), and Irene, who grew up on a farm near Chicago. The family moved to Texas when Emil took an executive position with Phillips Petroleum. Terry attended St. Stephen's Episcopal High School in Austin, where he performed in plays and became an outstanding football player in a state that prizes football. He attended Harvard University, where he studied philosophy with Stanley Cavell and graduated Phi Beta Kappa in 1965. He went on to become a Rhodes Scholar at Magdalen College, Oxford, but left before taking his doctorate, reportedly over a disagreement with his thesis adviser. He taught philosophy for a brief time at the Massachusetts Institute of Technology and, in 1969, published a translation of Martin Heidegger's *Vom Wessen des Grundes* (1929) as *The Essence of Reasons*. In the same year, however, he turned away from an academic career as a philosopher or a promising start as a freelance journalist (he had published a few articles in *Newsweek*, *Life*, and *The New Yorker*) to filmmaking, enrolling in the American Film Institute's brand-new conservatory, where one of his classmates was David Lynch. For his thesis project, Malick made *Lanton Mills*, a short starring Harry Dean Stanton and Warren Oates that almost no one has seen but that apparently evolved into his first feature screenplay credit, *Pocket Money* (1972), directed by Stuart Rosenberg. During his time at AFI, he also contributed to the scripts of *Deadhead Miles, Dirty Harry,* and *Drive, He Said*. Judging by the many contacts he quickly established, it was a good time to be an apprentice in a rapidly changing Hollywood, especially when you were lucky enough to have Michael Medavoy as an agent.

While acknowledging the originality of his talent, many critics have attempted to delineate the significant influences on Malick's film art. For obvious reasons, his training in philosophy, particularly his interest in Heidegger, has provided a persistent frame of reference, although not a particularly edifying one, if only because the German's ideas are difficult to tease out and frequently disputed. Cavell seems a more promising starting point, given his extended philosophy of film and the fact that he served as Malick's teacher at Harvard. Two of Cavell's most important concepts—as explicated in William Rothman and Marian Keane's excellent study of *The World Viewed*—seem to have had a major impact on Malick's filmmaking: the presentness of the world on film through our absence from it, and the correspondence between narrative film and myth. These theories help to account for the "visionary" or "poetic" qualities often found in the director's oeuvre and may help to illuminate certain privileged moments in specific films. The influence of American transcendentalism, and particularly Emerson, has already been suggested, although the authors of the sole book-length study of Malick to date, James Morrison and Thomas Schur, ignore Emerson completely while offering instead a rather baffling range of writers, including Flannery O'Connor, Willa Cather, Norman Mailer, and Henry James. They argue, unconvincingly, that "Malick wears his influences so much on his sleeve that they become something like floating signifiers" (29). Still others look to painters and filmmakers (especially the masters of the silent era) as sources.

Beyond these possible cultural progenitors, certain biographical circumstances provide tempting psychological clues to the inspiration behind Malick's recurrent themes and cinematic style. His sensitivity to the vagaries of nature and the autonomy of animals may be traced to his youthful summers working as a farm hand. His reported conflict with his senior tutor at Oxford, his many aborted film projects (beginning with being fired by Warners after working on a script that was the precursor for *Dirty Harry*), his conflicts with the producers of *Days of Heaven* and *The New World,* and, perhaps most significantly, his "terrible fights" with his father (Biskind, "Runaway" 206), suggest a habitual resistance to authority embodied in the alienated protagonists of his films. Set these cloudy biographical details aside: Malick remains a product of the late 1960s, of the civil rights movement, the Vietnam protests, Watergate, and the collapse of the Hollywood studio system. He has been academically trained to investigate complexity and question received truth. Is it any wonder, then, that his films have been shadowed by characters seeking refuge from civilization while engaged in various levels of metaphysical speculation?

The premature deaths of these rebellious or exiled figures may also have something to do with the tragedies that overtook both of Malick's younger brothers. Chris, the middle child, was terribly burned in an automobile accident that killed his wife. Larry, the youngest of the three Malick boys, traveled to Spain in 1968 to study guitar with the virtuoso Andrés Segovia. After bouts of depression, he broke his own hands and apparently committed suicide before his father could rescue him (Biskind, "Runaway" 206). It is perhaps too easy to suggest that the prominent scenes of fire marking every one of Malick's films reflect the memory of Chris's horrific experience or to suggest, as Simon Critchley has, that his male protagonists "are all somehow in love with death," but it also seems willfully obtuse not to consider the traumatic impact of these events on the older brother's developing sensibility.

Although he has cultivated the aura of a perfectionist and an isolated genius, Malick has demonstrated considerable entrepreneurial skills throughout his career, from self-financing his first feature, to raising big budgets ($52 million for *The Thin Red Line*) and then adhering to them for his comeback films, to producing independent films by younger directors. *Badlands* was independently produced on a budget of about $350,000 using a non-union crew. Warners purchased distribution rights for slightly less than a million dollars; the film took in a small profit at the box office but earned Malick excellent reviews and today is generally considered his most artistically successful film. In his influential *New*

Biographical Dictionary of Film, David Thomson begins his entry on Malick, "*Badlands* may be the most assured first film by an American since *Citizen Kane*" (566), extraordinary praise preserved in all subsequent editions. The movie may also be noteworthy because the director himself appears in a cameo speaking role as an architect looking for the wealthy homeowner whom Kit is holding hostage inside. In an ironic piece of business that befits the director's cryptic style, the visitor leaves a written message that Kit promptly discards, leaving the intended audience oblivious to its content. Prophetically, Malick's name does not appear as part of the cast in the film's closing credits.

Days of Heaven followed five years later, nearly two years of that time having been taken up with postproduction. Malick's visual virtuosity was again in evidence, earning Almendros his Oscar but angering Haskell Wexler, who felt he did not receive sufficient credit for his work after Almendros left to fulfill another assignment. Once more, a young female narrates the story of an outlaw couple on the run, leading some reviewers to criticize the director, unfairly, for repeating himself. The entire process of making *Days of Heaven*—ongoing disputes with the independent producers, Bert and Harold Schneider, conflicts on the set with Richard Gere, difficulties in editing the rough cut—proved exhausting and ultimately disillusioning when the film became a commercial failure, despite four Academy Award nominations and a generally favorable response. With an extended and apparently generous

contract for his future services from Paramount, Malick relocated to Paris sometime around 1979. Probably without his knowing it, his long hiatus from filmmaking had begun.

Rumors abound about his activities during this two-decade absence from public view, during which he evidently worked on a number of scripts that never made it to the screen. Perhaps the most intriguing of these projects was a treatment of the flamboyant 1950s rocker Jerry Lee Lewis that was rejected, although the biopic was ultimately filmed from an entirely different script as *Great Balls of Fire* (1989), directed by Jim McBride. The raw material of Lewis's story—a demonic, self-destructive musical prodigy, driven by ambition, jealousy, and lust, fulfills Kit Car-ruthers's unrequited dream to "sing a song about the way I feel" and make it a hit, then suddenly becomes a pariah—must have resonated with the expatriate director in the mid-1980s. Malick likely imagined a much darker and more beautiful film than the entertaining but shallow movie that was made.

Malick's reemergence as an auteur with Fox's announcement of pro-duction on *The Thin Red Line* provoked a buzz among cineastes, equaled only by Stanley Kubrick's return with *Eyes Wide Shut* a year later. In both cases, the movies that ensued proved to be less than masterpieces or popular successes, victims, perhaps, of their fans' unreasonable ex-pectations. Undoubtedly, *The Thin Red Line* suffered at the box office as a result of release of Steven Spielberg's World War II blockbuster *Saving Private Ryan* only a month earlier. Worldwide receipts for *The Thin Red Line* totaled a profitable $81 million, but that figure paled next to *Saving Private Ryan*'s $479 million (Flanagan 130). With its avoidance of the established generic tropes of the war film, multiple voiceovers, elliptical editing, metaphysical musings, and prolonged denouement, Malick's film seemed opaque compared to Spielberg's classical narrative and patriotic appeal to cultural memory. Nevertheless, reviews of *The Thin Red Line* were positive for the most part, respectful in nearly every case. The film was on the short list for many prestigious awards, includ-ing seven Academy Award nominations, and Malick won the New York Film Critics Circle Award for Best Director, but the overall response seemed to be: Good to have you back; better luck next time. Writing about the film a few years later and taking into account its "commercial underachievement" (130), Martin Flanagan wondered "if Malick, assuming he comes up with another project, [would be] entrusted with such resources again" (135).

He would be. New Line put up $40 million to produce *The New World*, Malick's meditation on the Pocahontas myth and the American Eden derived from a script he had written more than twenty years earlier. The film involves a paradoxical blend of historical re-creation—meticulously designed costumes and buildings on land in the immediate vicinity of the original Jamestown settlement, dialogue in the nearly extinct Algonquin language that the cast was required to learn—and romantic imagination, preserving the now-discredited love story between Smith and Pocahontas. Marketing this time focused less on the director than on his "discovery" of the film's star, the fifteen-year-old Peruvian Q'orianka Kilcher, who was chosen, New Line's publicity claims, from among three thousand actresses.

With the possible exception of cutting about seventeen minutes from the film's original two and half hours (edited from more than a million feet) immediately after its December 2005 release, Malick made even fewer concessions to the contemporary audience than he had in his previous epic. The pace of *The New World* is slow, the scenes without dialogue extended, the voiceovers abstract, the ending irresolute. Not surprisingly, domestic box-office receipts were disappointing, and reviews were decidedly more mixed than for any other previous Malick film. Critics seemed to be growing impatient with the director's visionary style, which felt "like poetry with too faint a pulse" to one reviewer (Denerstein). The Mexican cinematographer Emmanuel Lubezki received the picture's only Oscar nomination, and Kilcher won a few important acting awards, but the film slipped into DVD release without much notice.

Nevertheless, Malick seemed reenergized about the film industry in the new century, producing two independent features in 2004, David Gordon Green's *Undertow* and the very Malick-like *The Beautiful Country*, directed by Hans Petter Moland. He has recently been engaged in producing no fewer than three projects: Michael Apted's *Amazing Grace* (2006), an eighteenth-century thriller about the abolitionist William Wilberforce; Carlos Carrera's *The Marfa Lights*, a drama that takes place in Texas about twin brothers in conflict with their father(!); and Robert Redford's *Aloft*, based on Alan Tennant's book about tracking the peregrine falcon. In addition, he is scheduled to direct *The Tree of Life*, a version of his ambitious, unwieldy script "Q," which was first conceived in the 1970s. This latest project seems tentative at best, but Malick's fans await further news on the Internet with undiminished enthusiasm.

Badlands

Although the least officially honored at the time of its release, Malick's first film remains arguably the most perfectly realized of his four works to date. Its stature has grown through the years since its successful premiere at the 1973 New York Film Festival, as confirmed by its selection for the National Film Registry in 1993 and its inclusion in the AFI's list of the Four Hundred Greatest American Movies and *Sight and Sound's* 2002 list of films receiving votes for the British Film Institute (BFI) magazine's all-time Top Ten list. The writing, consisting mostly of Holly's extended narration and the largely phatic dialogue between the two young antiheroes, seems perfectly pitched to the banality and wanderlust of the characters. The cinematography is always carefully calculated and often breathtaking, the music uncanny and haunting, the performances among the most carefully modulated and yet affecting of Martin Sheen's and Sissy Spacek's sustained, distinguished careers. Curiously, *Badlands* might be the least dated of the director's four films.

The story is based on the notorious 1958 rampage of Charles Starkweather, a twenty-year-old dropout, and his fourteen-year-old girlfriend, Caril Ann Fugate. Before their capture, Starkweather managed to murder eleven victims in Nebraska and Wyoming, thereby initiating a kind of regional crisis in the American heartland soon to be exacerbated by the murder of the Clutter family in Holcomb, Kansas, a year later (immortalized in Truman Capote's *In Cold Blood* [1965] and Richard Brooks's film [1967]) and the 1966 shooting spree of the Texas Tower Sniper, Charles Whitman, who killed fifteen people and wounded thirty-one others on the campus of the University of Texas in Austin, Terry Malick's hometown. These three events within a period of eight years surrounding the Kennedy assassination in Dallas, each involving a young multiple murderer, shaped the consciousness of many American males of Malick's generation.

Unlike Brooks's *In Cold Blood*, *Badlands* does not use the actual criminals' names or closely adhere to the chain of events involved in the case, nor does it employ a documentary style, but Malick's film does retain enough of the basic details to be immediately recognizable in 1973 as a subjective adaptation of the Starkweather case. Sheen's Kit Carruthers seems slightly older and less of a punk than Charlie, but he dresses in the same denim jacket and jeans; wears his hair in a similar "hood" pompadour; works the same odd jobs, including time as a garbage man; and shares with the real-life killer a split personality, charming one moment but violent the next. Holly is also a bit older than Caril Ann, fifteen instead of fourteen, but otherwise embodies her passive acquiescence in the face of her boyfriend's violence. The geography is slightly altered—Nebraska becomes South Dakota, Wyoming becomes Montana—and the murders are reduced from eleven to five or seven (depending on whether you count the young couple in the storm cellar as victims), but the outlines of the actual circumstances are sufficiently in place to lend the events the character of myth. At the same time, Malick's expressionistic embellishments—the panoramic landscapes, montage sequences, ethereal musical themes, and hypnotic voiceover—add a dreamlike element to the characters' largely unmotivated behavior.

The film's other unmistakable source is Arthur Penn's *Bonnie and Clyde* (1967), an influence apparently acknowledged in the final credits, which thank Penn. Reviewers immediately noticed the parallels between the two movies about a young outlaw couple from a bygone era, and recent scholars like John Orr have continued to use Penn's classic as a touchstone for understanding *Badlands* ("Terrence Malick"). Indeed, it seems almost impossible to assess the original reception of Malick's film without taking into account the enormous critical and cultural impact of its predecessor, and it is hard even today to watch the exploits of Kit and Holly without simultaneously thinking about Bonnie and Clyde. The elements of homage in *Badlands* deliberately invite an intertextual reading: as in *Bonnie and Clyde,* the opening shot of *Badlands* depicts the female lead reclining on her brass bed; as their crime sprees spread, both insecure male outlaws find self-validation in celebrity; Bonnie's proud self-introduction ("We rob banks") is echoed in Kit's ("Name's Carruthers. Believe I shoot people every now and then"); in both films, the courtship begins with a walk down the desultory main street of a sleepy town; the loving relationships in each case are shadowed by a form of sexual dysfunction; after the first murder, Kit offers to go it alone

("You want to call the police, it's fine. Just won't be so hot for me"), just as Clyde had offered to put Bonnie on a bus straight back to West Dallas, both killers thereby testing the loyalty of their girlfriends; the climactic car chase across the prairie in *Badlands* clearly reflects several similar escapades in *Bonnie and Clyde*; both men offer to buy their partners a fancy meal as reward for their companionship; both films are marked by a dark fatality and punctuated by an original musical score.

These similarities, however, only highlight the more profound differences between *Badlands* and *Bonnie and Clyde,* contrasts that suggest how Malick deliberately deconstructs Penn's take on the American culture of violence. Most apparently, *Badlands* utterly lacks the energy and high-spiritedness of the earlier film. Although he may be equally illiterate and sexually inept, Clyde Barrow possesses a sincerity and capacity for loving care nearly absent in Kit's personality (except for the moment of genuine feeling when he dances to "A Blossom Fell"). In contrast to Bonnie's intense longing, Holly's quest for romantic fulfillment seems dreary and passionless. A listlessness pervades *Badlands,* registered in the detachment of Holly's narration and Kit's recurrent sighs, that resonates all the more deeply when measured against the exuberance of the first two-thirds of *Bonnie and Clyde.* Compare, for example, Holly's telling of the dumb joke about the naked man who wore only hat and gloves with Buck's twice-told tale in *Bonnie and Clyde* that ends with the punch line, "Don't sell that cow!" Buck "sells" the joke through his sheer conviction about its funniness; Holly, by contrast, is an inexperienced joke teller telling an even more moronic joke.

Unlike Penn's antiheroes, Malick's outlaw couple has no sense of family or class solidarity—they are no Robin Hoods; they are not plagued by memories of relatives left behind—nor do they seem to be redeemed or even uplifted by sexual consummation. Six years after Penn was criticized for romanticizing the criminality of the Barrow Gang and splattering the screen with unprecedented gore, Malick treats his protagonists as apathetic, pathological outsiders—not "beautiful losers," to borrow the enduring title of Leonard Cohen's 1966 novel—and depicts Kit's violence as reflexive, meaningless, "deadening" in every sense. None of the murder scenes involves gore or significant suffering. By divesting his protagonists of glamor and denying them any significant psychological depth, by rendering their crimes pointless and their behavior incomprehensible, by depicting violence as idiomatic rather than shocking and love as performative rather than self-fulfilling, Malick effectively modifies the cycle of anti-establishment road movies aimed at a young audience that began with *Bonnie and Clyde* and *Easy Rider* (1969). The exuberant rebelliousness of the late 1960s seems to have given way to the enervated solipsism of the early 1970s. The paradoxical opacity that was to become Malick's signature—the more we see, the less we understand—begins with *Badlands*: no one, it seems, can express what it all "means."

Voiceover Narration: Holly and Tom Sawyer

Normatively, cinematic voiceover serves as an explanatory device. The film's opening image and Holly's expository narration thus are calculated to encourage spectators to regard the film as a bildungsroman, the Dickensian story of an innocent young girl's passage into adult experience: "My mother died of pneumonia when I was just a kid. My father had kept his wedding cake in a freezer for ten whole years. After the funeral, he gave it to the yard man. He tried to be cheerful, but he could never be consoled by the little stranger he found in his house. Then one day, hoping to begin a new life away from the scene of all his memories, he moved us from Texas to Fort Dupree, South Dakota."

Holly's adventure, however, brings neither meaningful insight nor newfound articulateness ("It all goes to show how you can know a person and not really know them," she opines after Kit shoots his final victims). Once Kit drives away from the burning house, the film takes on the features of a different popular genre, but Jonathan Bignell correctly points out how "the journey in *Badlands* undercuts assumptions about self-discovery in the road movie" (42). Kit, like Holly, never understands his own motives or expresses remorse for his crimes. Asked by a lawman following his capture why he did it, he can only reply, "I always wanted to be a criminal, I guess. Just not this big a one." Comparing *Badlands* to two other contemporary movies with strikingly similar plots, *Thieves Like Us* (dir. Robert Altman, 1974) and *The Sugarland Express* (dir. Steven Spielberg, 1974), Marsha Kinder emphasizes the relatively unappealing shallowness of Holly's character, making it virtually impossible to identify with or to interpret her behavior. "She is shrouded in the kind of ambiguity that surrounds Patty Hearst—is she merely a passive victim who has been dragged along by her criminal captors, or has she been romantically transformed and infected by the outlaw mentality?" (7). Penn makes the distinction clear in *Bonnie and Clyde*; Malick leaves the question rhetorical in *Badlands*.

The banality of Holly's voiceover commentary and the disturbing flatness of its inflection, "both diegetic and metadiegetic at the same time" (McGettigan, "Interpreting" 34), serve to compound the film's thematic ambiguity: not simply the more we see but the more we *hear*, it turns out, the less we understand. Her responses to the events she describes consistently prove insufficient, as if Nancy Drew were narrating *Hiroshima, Mon Amour* (dir. Alain Resnais, 1959). She reveals in the last words of her opening monologue that she is talking about an episode in her life now closed, distanced from her current role as storyteller: "Little did I realize that what began in the alleys and backways of this quiet town would end in the Badlands of Montana." This laconic tone persists to the end, when she describes her own fate, presently far removed in time and space from her notorious past: "Myself, I got off with probation and a lot of nasty looks. Later, I married the son of the lawyer who defended me." Unlike the vernacular insights often spoken by Linda, the child narrator of *Days of Heaven*, or the musings of several soldiers on the sound track of *The Thin Red Line*, Holly's commentary consists almost exclusively of platitudes and clichés ("Better to spend a week with one who loved me for what I was than years of loneliness"), sometimes creating unintended humor ("In the stench and slime of the feed lot, he'd remember how I looked the night before") or incomprehensible non-sequiturs ("The whole time the only thing I did wrong was throwing out my fish when he got sick. Later I got a new one, but this incident kept on bothering me"). While the intensity of Emmanuelle Riva's narration in *Hiroshima, Mon Amour* derives from her capacity to conjure up historical images and forbidden desires, to relive them in her act of enunciation, Holly's monotone becomes haunting rather than boring precisely because she herself seems so unhaunted by memory (Michaels 145–46). She is, by the end of the diegesis and the beginning of her narration, "less traumatized by her experience than abstracted from it" (Zaller 148).

A different analogy might help to define Holly's distinctive persona as the film's narrator: she is like Tom Sawyer but without his vitality and charm, or "personality," as she calls it. Both young small-town characters remain, despite their misbehavior, ultimately pliant and conservative, recognizable as "good delinquents" eager to please and readily reabsorbed into society. Their language and attitude have already been determined by popular culture (Tom's adventure stories, Holly's schoolbooks and romance magazines) and an ingrained sense of propriety. Holly's empty gestures—chatting with the dying Cato, commiserating with the girlfriend in the Studebaker, complimenting the rich man, waiting for Kit to open the car door for her—carry no more significance than Tom's elaborate machinations for "freeing" the already-liberated Jim at the end of *The Adventures of Huckleberry Finn*.

At various points, Holly's voiceover also adopts the "literary" style of teenage romances, travelogues, or, in the forest sequence, *The Swiss Family Robinson*. As is true for the narrators of Malick's subsequent films, she views events from the perspective not of one who has initiated the action but of one who is "taken along, as it were, for the ride" (McGettigan, "Interpreting" 33). In the context of today's reportage, we might call her an *embedded* narrator, although her credibility—but never her veracity—is frequently called into question by the images themselves. Thus, she dutifully reports Kit's account of his deadly encounter with the posse: "Kit felt bad about shooting those men in the back, but he said they'd come in like that and they would have played it down and dirty as they could, and besides, he'd overheard them whispering about how they were only interested in the reward money. With lawmen it would have been different. They were out there to get a job done and they deserved a fair chance. But not a bounty hunter."

But the camera shows three uniformed men and no conversation about reward money. When Holly later voices suspicion about Kit's version of his capture and the images of the final moments of the car chase confirm her doubts, we can measure at least some growth in her perceptions. At other times, her commentary seems simply incommensurate with the grandeur or acuteness of the imagery, as when she describes, *Kon Tiki*–style, how "there wasn't a plant in the forest that didn't come in handy," and a montage of five micro-close-ups displays images of isolated natural beauty that supersede her field-guide pragmatism. "When words and images absolutely contradict each other," Wheeler Dixon writes in his study of cinematic depictions of Eden, "the images always seem to be the truth tellers" (114). The sublime quality of the film's arcadian vision in this sequence belies the borrowed language Holly employs to describe the scene.

"A Cinema of Poetry"

The cinematography throughout *Badlands* continually serves in this same way as counterpoint to Holly and Kit's quotidian observations but also, especially when the long lens is employed, as a means of reinforcing their shallow and static qualities. The lack of depth registered by the telephoto shots thus contributes to a perception of literal flatness in the characters, who sometimes appear strangely removed from their surroundings. When Kit introduces himself to Holly in the opening scene, for example, she appears against the blurred background of leafy trees immediately behind her, thereby appearing to stand apart from the natural world. Later, the telephoto long shots of the stolen Cadillac speeding towards the camera across the plains create the illusion of movement without progress, providing a visual equivalent to the runaway couple's unchanging circumstances. When, at the rich man's house, Holly describes how "the world was like a faraway planet to which I could never return," the long lens again underscores her sense of detachment and the spectator's own distance from her underdeveloped consciousness. "The effect is the creation of a perceiving sensibility that seems interested in everything and affected by nothing" (Shepard 45). The

vast vacancy of the northern prairie, framed repeatedly in long shots reminiscent of John Ford's landscapes of Monument Valley, becomes at these moments an objective correlative for the vacuity of Malick's protagonists, a geographical and psychological emptiness the director nonetheless treats with profound respect.

The discrepancy between Malick's "perceiving sensibility" and that of his characters may be best represented in the remarkable construction of Kit's initial meeting with Holly's father (Warren Oates), who is painting a billboard in the midst of a flat, deserted area outside of town. Malick dissolves from the second floor of a building where Holly takes clarinet lessons to this previously unseen (and unsuspected) place, without a highway or even road in sight. There is a self-reflexive element to the mise-en-scène here: the billboard resembles a drive-in movie screen, with Holly's father in the process of filling in the details of a verdant "long shot" of an archetypal domestic space, yellow house, green yard, not unlike the first carefully composed shots of Holly's yellow Victorian home. In this way, the sign painter as "artist" is linked to the film's director (Oates had acted in Malick's AFI short, *Lanton Mills*), two skillful craftsmen filling in a huge frame with generically similar images but with vastly different ambitions. Following social conventions, Kit in effect asks her father for Holly's hand in a series of shot/countershots that employ sharp angles to reflect the older man's elevated point of view as well as the apparent power relationship in the dialogue. Holly's father is seen through a lens that reduces his separation from the painting behind him and keeps the background images in sharp focus. The billboard, we can now see, is a kind of paint-by-numbers "Peaceable Kingdom," with house, garden, farm animals, fish-stocked pond, and sky painted in a totally flat perspective. When the unsuccessful "proposal" ends, Malick concludes the sequence with an extreme long shot—what normally might be the establishing shot—of the billboard and Mr. Sargis's Jeep set off against the endless plains and the same blue sky with puffy white clouds depicted in the sign, then holds the shot for an extra beat. The surrealistic effect of this scene—like a Magritte painting, incongruous and self-referential—lingers well beyond its diegetic significance, suggesting something akin to Holly's later description of the world being "like a faraway planet."

In the billboard sequence and throughout *Badlands* (the formally

composed landscape of the couple playing cards under a spreading tree beside the river may serve as another example), Malick extends Pier Paolo Pasolini's conception of "the double register of the cinema of poetry, the subject's disturbed vision of the world and, by substitution, the director's artistic representation of it" (Orr, "Cinema" 134), to suggest the dissociated personalities of the film's protagonists. In at least two other ways, the film's associational structure (analogous to rhyme) and its symbol making (as with the billboard), *Badlands* exemplifies the poetic sensibility frequently ascribed to its creator. Instead of character development or turning points in the plot, Malick shapes the film by repeating certain images, giving them an inexpressible weight and formally organizing the narrative as an alternative to Holly's inchoate voiceover. Thus, early in the film, he shows us five dogs—Holly's black and white dog on her bed, the dead "collie" on the garbage route, the barking dog that Kit quiets with a piece of fruit, the foreman's dog when Kit is fired, and again Holly's dog before and after her dad shoots it—then adds another in the background at the rich man's house as a reminder of the world the couple has left behind. The opening image of Holly lying on her brass bed is followed thirteen minutes later by a similar shot of Kit, the camera once more tracking back to reveal the brass bedstead.

Having established an associative rhythm, *Badlands* proceeds through a series of binary repetitions: two dances ("Love Is Strange" and "A Blossom Fell"), two testaments (the record left at the fire and the Dictaphone message at the rich man's house), two boxes of relics (one sent aloft and the other buried), two white hats (Holly's father's and the rich man's Panama, which Kit appropriates). Kit's parting words to Holly's father at the billboard, "Takes all kinds," becomes a self-explanatory refrain when he replies to the lawmen with the identical phrase after his capture. Similarly, his threatening phrase, "Suppose I shot you? How'd that be?" is echoed in more polite tones but with the same gun in hand to the rich man: "We'd like to hang out here for a while. How'd that be?" The lyrical moment early in the film when Kit launches a balloon containing "a box with some of our tokens and things" is duplicated in the denouement, when the light plane ascends with the two prisoners aboard. In most narratives, such repetitions serve as markers for critical changes in the characters and their circumstances, as in the three scaffold scenes of Hawthorne's *The Scarlet Letter* or the three appearances of the green light at the end of the dock in Fitzgerald's *The Great Gatsby*. In *Badlands*, however, these motifs seem to measure only the director's sensibility and say nothing about any heightened consciousness in the two protagonists.

Some images, of course, like the white hats, convey fairly clear, even allegorical meanings. The beautiful, much admired fire sequence, a prominent visual element in each of Malick's four films, serves as the story's turning point, a kind of "narrative caesura" (Zaller 141) initiating the couple's career as fugitives, and, accompanied by swelling choral music, as a transcendent spectacle rich in symbolism and suggestiveness. Other overdetermined details, like the billboard, resonate without being indicative of any certain value. Take the moment, for example, near the end of their flight when Kit shoots a football that, Holly reports, "he considered excess baggage." This image rhymes with two earlier long shots: the view of Kit stepping on a dead steer in the feed lot, and the scene in the river when, having failed to catch a fish with a makeshift net, he tries to shoot it in the water. Each of these three interludes briefly calls into question Kit's state of mind, if not his sanity.

The "dead" football remains the most melancholy and disturbing variation, a metaphor for Kit's deflated dreams, like his habitual sighs. While he methodically knocks the air out of the pigskin as he earlier poked at the diseased steer, the visual association reflects the entropy that has overcome him and that culminates when he shoots the tire of his getaway car before surrendering. His violence has become merely reflexive, another empty gesture rather than a heroic stand for young love against parental authority or even an imagined act of self-defense. A few minutes later, after he dryly suggests that they might have hopped a speeding train, Holly replies, "You're crazy!" His act of shooting a football could be said to provoke a similar response from the numbed movie audience. Is Kit, after all, simply "off his bean" and the film a case study of his gradual breakdown? Through such "poetic" moments, Malick makes it difficult to judge his characters because it is impossible to understand them. The sad mystery of *Badlands* emanates from Kit's and Holly's limited self-awareness and arrested responsiveness, conveyed through the vacancy of the vast landscape that so often surrounds them.

Identity and "Character"

Beyond her opening monologue and a few contradictory glimpses of interactions with her father (the relationship seems healthy when he playfully squirts her with a paint brush, then troubled when he methodically shoots her dog as punishment for secretly hanging out with Kit), Malick provides no psychological insights into Holly's character. She mentions her parents only once after they are gone and hardly seems traumatized—merely frightened—when Kit murders her father before her eyes. Her only reaction at the time is to slap him, perhaps the only gesture she knows to register her sense of personal violation.

Kit reveals even less of his background than Holly in her opening monologues: the only hint about his past is a barely audible comment about "Korea" he makes while he and Holly are making out under the bleachers. The subsequent scenes of him drilling with his rifle in the forest and his evident marksmanship in gunning down Cato suggest that he may have served his country in that conflict—although this biographical speculation cannot be confirmed. As Holly remains a cipher (at various times, Kit refers to her as "Red," "Priscilla," "Tex," and "Mildred," each time without drawing a reply), Kit seems equally in search of a viable identity. His self-image derives from his supposed resemblance to James Dean, a double whom he imitates poorly on those occasions when he behaves politely towards his elders (addressing Mr. Sargis as "sir," apologizing to the rich man for "barging in" on his home) or has time to rehearse valedictory speeches for his imagined admirers ("Listen to your parents and teachers. They got a line on most things. Try to keep an open mind. Consider the minority opinion, but try to get along with the majority of opinion once it's accepted"). Empty of identity, they both try out different roles, illustrated in Holly's putting on eye makeup in the forest or wearing the lace shawl she finds at the rich man's house and in Kit's dreams of being a "cowboy" while working in the feed lot or joining the Royal Canadian Mounted Police. Brian Henderson has suggested that this compulsive role playing combined with their habit of collecting souvenirs and other useless objects (like the football) represents "an 'existential' view of character" (39), one that begins with nothing essential.

This confusion of being with role playing runs through all four of Malick's features: Abby and Bill pose as brother and sister; Colonel Tall represses his true feelings for the sake of career, playing the hardened soldier; Pocahontas impersonates an "English" wife without ever losing her Native American soul. Kit remains the most disturbing and pathetic of these poseurs, a "bad actor" in the literal sense of being unconvincing and the colloquial meaning of displaying a sinister charm. Eventually, even Holly can see through his performance, becoming progressively bored by his patter. From beginning to end, he is recognized by others merely as a "character" ("You sumpthin'," Mr. Sargis tells him at the end of their conversation, a phrase echoed by the deputy's compliment about his individuality in the closing scene). Only in the hollow celebrity briefly afforded by his apprehension does he seem to find personal fulfillment. Watching over the dying Cato, locking the young couple into the storm cellar, turning over a list of "borrowed" items to the rich man, car swapping with the oil driller, he continually plays "the affable man with the gun" (Shepard 41), less the rebel without a cause than a kind of frontier Hollow Man. Malick brilliantly suggests this particular association with T. S. Eliot's poetry in the telephoto long shot of Kit looking like a scarecrow with a rifle slung over his shoulders gazing at the distant horizon during "the magic hour," a composition frequently cited as a cinematic allusion to Dean's last role in George Stevens's *Giant* (1956).

Sensing his own insubstantiality perhaps, Kit repeatedly attempts to memorialize his experiences: saving a rock as a souvenir of the couple's first lovemaking, launching a balloon containing a packet of their "little tokens and things," burying another bucket of trinkets that "somebody might dig up in a thousand years and wouldn't they wonder," building a

cairn to mark the spot where he is captured, doling out personal effects to the lawmen, and twice preserving his voice by making homemade recordings. In these gestures he takes up the task of Eliot's persona in "The Waste Land" ("These fragments I have shored against my ruins"), but to no enduring effect. "These little monuments are attempts to mark space and to fix meaning," Bignell has suggested, "but they remain heaps of rocks and a bucket of dusty bric-a-brac" (46).

Kit's relationship with Holly turns out to be equally barren of significance: she is simply his "girl," as he introduces her to Cato, someone to "scream out his name" when he dies, thereby confirming his movie hero's role. The pastoral setting for their initial lovemaking and the post-coital question about its success may evoke Clyde Barrow's long-delayed consummation of his love for Bonnie, but Malick depicts it without psychological nuance or romantic appeal. "Gosh, what was everyone talking about?" Holly wonders. Despite Kit's courteous or protective gestures and Holly's efforts to describe themselves as being "like any couple," their relations remain strangely impersonal, never more so than when Holly is transported by the vistas in her stereopticon.

This scene, her last moment of tranquility during their sojourn in the forest, serves as the most sustained insight into Holly's dissociated personality and as the film's most self-consciously reflexive moment. As she gazes at a montage of seven antique images—a tree-lined canal in Rio de Janeiro, the Sphinx, a mountain river with a steamboat in the background, a mother and child, a color-tinted portrait of two women at a piano, a large family gathering on the lawn, a young cavalry officer kissing a shy girl—her voiceover focuses on a series of questions regarding the future. "It hit me that I was just this little girl, born in Texas, whose father was a sign painter, who had just only so many years to live. It sent a chill down my spine, and I thought: where would I be this very moment if Kit had never met me? Or killed anybody? This very moment. If my mom had never met my dad? If she had never died? And what's the man I'll marry gonna look like? What's he doing this very minute? Is he thinking about me now, by some coincidence, even though he doesn't know me? Does it show on his face?"

The pictures themselves have little in common except for the period in which they were taken. They can roughly be dated around the turn of the twentieth century, thereby corresponding with the invention of the film apparatus, and their appeal to Holly parallels that of the original "cinema of attractions," an opportunity to view faraway places previously inaccessible to provincial audiences. Malick compounds this analogy to watching film by foregrounding the process of montage, by including the tinted image (simulating a technique of early cinema), and by introducing the conspicuous zoom on the final shot of the young couple. The sound track, from Carl Orff's "Musica Poetica," further sets off the sequence from immediate reality. Holly's dreamy narration, of course, may also reflect the viewer's rapture in the contemplation of the flow of images. The cinematic presentation of the stereopticon vistas, in other words, allows Malick to direct his audience's attention to their own act of *watching*.

Holly's speculations anticipate the increasingly complex meditations on human destiny in the voiceovers of Malick's subsequent films. While her contemplations can be expressed only in clichés ("It sent a chill down my spine"), the impulse to pierce life's mysteries and to assert one's place in some preordained future remains a constant theme among the more expressive protagonists to come. But while the inner thoughts of the girl Linda, Private Witt, and Captain Smith suggest a heightened sensitivity to their own experiences, Holly's monologue here sends a chill because it remains so far removed from her current situation. Although she has said, "I sensed that my destiny now lay with Kit," a short time earlier, she now seems to have forgotten him—despite his presence in the background

of the scene's establishing shot—as she focuses on the cavalry soldier's romantic kiss. This kind of distanciation in a literary text usually allows for rhetorical grace and narrative interpretation, but Holly's fanciful musings suggest only vacuity, her profound out-of-it-ness.

Misguided Ambition, Unrequited Dreams

Despite Kit's pathological behavior and Holly's maddening propriety, despite their shared shallowness, inarticulateness, and anomie, despite the film's refusal to impute psychological or political motivations for their crimes, Malick never appears to mock or even dismiss his characters any more than he attempts to glorify them. While he deconstructs the myth of the movie antihero that reached an apotheosis between *Bonnie and Clyde* and *The Godfather* (1972), he paradoxically invests Kit and Holly with a kind of mythic innocence. Kit may shoot his only friend, Cato, in the back, but he politely holds the screen door open for him and, along with Holly, engages the dying man in small talk. No hard feelings, he seems to say. As Holly lapses into reverie with her stereopticon, she pictures herself as the virginal bride-to-be of the photograph. Bonnie Parker also indulges this fantasy of starting a new, "clean" life before Clyde inadvertently brings her back to the reality of her inescapable past, but Holly's imagined future remains untainted by her association with Kit. In contrast to the lyrics of "A Blossom Fell," for her the romantic dream has not ended; in fact, in the future from which she narrates the film, it has been fulfilled ("I married the son of the lawyer who defended me").

Kit also achieves a form of self-fulfillment during the denouement of *Badlands* merely by becoming the center of attention. Unlike the mythic figures of classic American road movies—gangster, homesteader, prospector, immigrant—Kit is not out for material gain or career advancement ("the big score" that Bill pursues in *Days of Heaven*); instead, his dream is only to be recognized. The notoriety he achieves during the manhunt gives way to the celebrity of his airport sendoff, which Malick constructs as a parodic presidential press conference or movie premiere with Kit as its star. He signs legal documents and hands out the pen as a souvenir, passes out other personal items as treasured keepsakes, and ingratiatingly responds to questions from the young lawmen who have become his fans. All the while the camera keeps him in the center of the frame, with his captors either on the periphery or offscreen. "Boy, we rang the bell, didn't we?" he proudly confides to Holly.

Kit thus becomes the first of Malick's delusional or misguided adventurers, though the objective of his quest turns out to be the least substantial of all. Jim Shepard likens him to the Western hero of Robert Warshow's seminal essay on the topic, a man (so unlike Captain Smith of *The New World*) not seeking new dominions but attempting to preserve a dignified way of life, to act out the role of "cowboy" or "Mountie" instead of being labeled a garbage man. "It wasn't violence at all that was the point," Shepard says of the Westerner, "but a certain image, a style, which expressed itself most clearly in violence" (41). Violence is certainly the point in celebrated American movies like *Bonnie and Clyde, The Wild Bunch* (1969), and *The Godfather,* which suggests one reason for the disorienting impact of the bloodless murders in *Badlands.* Malick seems more interested in the criminal couple's state of mind—their ontology, if you will—than in the visceral causes and effects of their violence.

Kit's restless yearning for a mythically innocent past, epitomized in his expression of something close to rapture while listening to Nat King Cole and performed in his polite gestures and respect for elders, finds its echo in Holly's voiceover, whose presiding impulse is to please her listeners. Her refusal to confront the unpleasantness of her experience may be understood (as Malick himself seems to have understood it [see the interview with Beverly Walker in this volume]) not as moronic or evasive but as her untutored effort to appeal to a 1950s audience steeped in popular romances. Kit, after all, "was handsomer than anybody I'd ever met" and "loved me for what I was." She is never more credible, despite such platitudinous sentiments, than when she describes how each of them "lived for the precious hours when he or she could be with the other, away from all the cares of the world." Every one of Malick's four films is suffused with a similar longing for an irrecoverable moment of untroubled isolation, here the interlude in the forest.

The nostalgia that suffuses *Badlands* seems particularly complicated. The sentimentality of Holly's narration and the conservatism underlying Kit's pathology, their mutual conformity ("Kit made me get my books from school so I wouldn't fall behind"), might be paralleled by the audience's impulse to label them as types and to categorize the film by genre—efforts likely to fail because, unlike his protagonists, Malick is not trying to please. In 1973, perhaps, the mythic innocence that was the staple product of the classical Hollywood cinema seemed as distant to a serious director as the Canadian Rockies to the runaways.

Badlands marks a ritualized end to innocence in the fire sequence that follows the murder of Holly's father. Holly leaves the house carrying only a small suitcase and a framed painting, which can be identified later in the tree house as a landscape by Albert Bierstadt, whose representations of the frontier strongly influenced popular conceptions of the American West as a place of pristine beauty, a Paradise regained. Before lighting the fuse, Kit plays his "suicide" recording, which lamely justifies his crime: "He was provoking me when I popped him." The montage of fire that follows, consisting of twenty carefully edited shots accompanied by a chorus of sacred music, was justly praised in many contemporary reviews. Malick's camera seems remarkably close to the burning cauldron, creating a sense of imminent danger to be repeated in *Days of Heaven* and capturing several striking images from the interior of the house. In a series of three shots, each successively closer, he shows Holly's brass bed with a doll lying on the covers being consumed in flames, then cuts to a close-up of a collapsing doll house, followed by other views of the piano and other furniture being swallowed up in the conflagration, all signifying an end to childhood. The fire sequence maintains an awful beauty throughout the scene, even in the close shot of Mr. Sargis's body on the cellar floor, the flames leaping in the background, destroying forever the Norman Rockwell image of domestic tranquility inscribed by the film's initial long shot of the house. Malick concludes this transitional part of the narrative with a final bit of virtuosity: a gorgeous match dissolve from the blacktop leading diagonally out of town to the river in the forest, while the sound track switches to Erik Satie's music and the resumption of Holly's voiceover describing their new life in the wilderness.

From this point on, Holly's story shifts from romance to captivity tale, another woman's genre, as she describes surviving the hardships

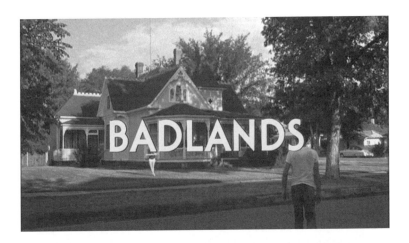

of a primitive, precarious existence, finally to be rescued and returned to civilization (Shepard 47). Like the original captivity narratives, hers has an ambivalent subtext, the effect of which can be registered in her barely perceptible smile at the film's conclusion. Although she becomes increasingly distressed by her primitive existence ("I feel kinda like an animal living out here," she complains), collaborates with her rescuers, and accepts readmission into society, some part of her has enjoyed the ride, as her detailed act of retelling it ultimately testifies. She has learned her lesson, though: "I made up my mind never to tag along with the hell-bent type."

What lessons remain for the audience of *Badlands*? Malick, as has been suggested, makes certain that his meaning cannot be so glibly expressed. In his avoidance of psychological or ideological explanations for narrative events, in fact, the director stands outside the usual practice of the New Hollywood. Although irony and detachment have become the hallmarks of a modernist sensibility, the distancing effects of *Badlands* have nothing to do with a condescending or satirical attitude towards the characters. Holly herself is incapable of irony: when Kit makes his remark about hopping a fast train, she replies, "It was going too fast." When she comments about how "nice" their secluded rendezvous by the river is, he confirms her aesthetic judgment, "It's the tree that makes it nice." The impulse to laugh, ingrained in audiences since *Bonnie and Clyde* and *Butch Cassidy and the Sundance Kid* (1969), dies with recognition of the characters' sincerity. "I'm serious," Holly insists near the end of their journey when Kit tries to ignore her complaints. To take Malick's protagonists seriously means to respect their yearnings and to acknowledge their despair, but it does not mean that their alienation can be attributed to social injustice, as is true for so many films of the period. *Badlands'* "feeling of detachment hinges in part on a distinct indifference to the social-problem dimensions of the material. Kit and Holly are seen as significant neither as menaces to social welfare nor as representatives of social pathology" (Morrison and Shur 17). In each successive film, Malick will gradually augment the ideological implications, but in *Badlands* the contesting claims of alienated youth and established society seem to cancel each other. Thus, the audience can identify neither with Kit's paranoia and victim mentality ("Bet they'll blame that on me," he complains while passing a roadside wreck. "Bastards!") nor with the self-righteous vigilantes of the monochromatic newsreel montage or National Guardsmen spread across the widescreen at the airport.

In *Badlands,* Malick, a philosopher who has denied the possibility of filming philosophy, begins his lifelong aesthetic quest (perhaps again influenced by Heidegger) to depict the autonomous *being* of persons and things. His response to those reviewers and critics who have continually questioned this artistic ambition and likened his style to the obscurantism of the European art film might be to paraphrase the poet Archibald MacLeish's celebrated aphorism (in "Ars Poetica"): A (Malick) film should not mean, but be.

Days of Heaven

Malick's second feature had a long and, by most accounts, difficult gestation. The arduous shoot in Alberta was marked by ongoing disputes between the director and his producers, the estimable Bert and Harold Schneider (who had previously collaborated on such significant independent films as *Five Easy Pieces, The Last Picture Show,* and *The King of Marvin Gardens*). Malick also wrangled with Richard Gere, hired for his first starring role after John Travolta, Al Pacino, and Dustin Hoffman reportedly turned down the part. Malick's perfectionism, already established after *Badlands,* became legendary with *Days of Heaven.* He virtually scrapped his own script and improvised many scenes on location, repeatedly changed the shooting schedule (thereby irritating the crew, comprised mostly of seasoned Hollywood professionals), instructed the production designer Jack Fisk to build an entire mansion, inside and outside, instead of the customary façade, then spent two years agonizing over the editing decisions, a process that would have been intolerable in the Old Hollywood. When Nestor Almendros had to leave the production to honor a prior commitment, the great American cinematographer Haskell Wexler was brought in to complete the work, resulting in a remarkably seamless look to the completed picture but ultimately angering Wexler when Almendros won the Oscar and he was relegated to an "additional cinematography" credit. To this day, Wexler claims that at least half the final footage is his (Ebert).

Something of a sea change had occurred in American cinema in the five years between *Badlands* and the premiere of *Days of Heaven* in

1978. With the enormous success of Steven Spielberg's *Jaws* (1975) and George Lucas's *Star Wars* (1977), film audiences began to turn away from the "independent" products of the new American auteurs and embraced the high-concept, special-effects blockbusters that marked a new era. Against this shifting cultural taste, *Days of Heaven*, with its formal beauty, simple plot, lyrical interludes, and ambiguous theme, seemed heavy-handed and pretentious to many viewers but brilliant to as many others. Contemporary reviews were decidedly mixed, with several of the most influential critics weighing in negatively: Pauline Kael described it as "all visual bombast" (447); the *New York Times* reviewer, Harold Schonberg, called it "an intolerably artsy, artificial film"; Andrew Sarris branded "'its drama deficient, and its psychology obscure'" (qtd. in Petric 37); and David Denby, in the harshest notice, found it "'one of the most perversely undramatic, uninvolving, and senseless movies ever made'" (qtd. in Petric 37). These reviews prompted the Harvard scholar Vlada Petric to write a spirited defense in a lengthy review in *Film Quarterly* ("It seems preposterous that some critics overlook the *cinematic* function of the visual beauty" [43]), and *Days of Heaven* went on to win several distinguished awards, reaping four Academy Award nominations (including Almendros's Oscar) and Best Director prizes for Malick at Cannes and from the New York Film Critics Circle.

Scholars and cineastes remain divided over *Days of Heaven*. David Thomson, for example, regards it as "a very disappointing follow up" to *Badlands* (567), while Peter Biskind sees it as "a dark jewel of a film" ("Runaway" 204). The authors of the first book-length study of the director apparently side with Thomson, deciding that "*Badlands* is the kind of film that gets made fortuitously when new possibilities—styles, powers, forces—are on the rise, and *Days of Heaven* is the kind that gets made after those possibilities have become entrenched" (Morrison and Schur 101). Following the line of Petric's rejoinder, the debate continues to revolve around what to make of "its extremities of beauty" (Cavell xiv), whether the exquisite lighting, painterly compositions, dreamy dissolves, and fluid camera movements, combined with the epic grandeur and elegiac tone, sufficiently compensate for the thinness of the tale, the two-dimensionality of the characters, and the resulting emotional detachment of the audience. What may be most interesting about these polarizing opinions is that they remain in place today, when critics regard Malick's now-doubled body of work. Few American directors have inspired such adulation and rejection with each successive film.

Despite its idiosyncratic qualities, *Days of Heaven* belongs to a group of highly regarded movies of the era that, in a variety of ways, sought to transform the American epic: *The Godfather, The Godfather, Part II* (1974), *Nashville* (1975), *The Deer Hunter* (1978), *Apocalypse Now* (1979), *Heaven's Gate* (1980). The film's concern with certain national myths—particularly the migration westward, the dream of personal success, and the clash of agrarian and industrial economies—pervades nearly every scene, but unlike these other films, *Days of Heaven* remains ideologically neutral in depicting what seems the fated course of events. In his return to a version of the Western, for example, Malick "does not so much disprove the myth of the West as demonstrate our need for it and reinforce our desire for it" (McGettigan, "*Days*" 51). He has little regard for geographical verisimilitude (most obviously in substituting Alberta for the Texas Panhandle but also by placing herds of buffalo amidst endless acres of wheat in 1916) or historical specificity (most obviously in Gere's modern hairstyle but also in several anachronistic phrases like Bill's "big federal case!"). Nor does he portray the Farmer as an insensitive capitalist tyrant or the migrant workers as oppressed victims. Instead, the narrative vacillates between an elegiac paean to a lost harmony with nature and a prophetic vision of national apocalypse, with the epilogue further complicating the tragic dimensions of the plot.

Most reviewers and audiences at the time immediately placed *Days of Heaven* in the context of the director's previous work, implicitly acknowledging Malick as an American auteur after only two features. Like *Badlands*, the new film relates the devolving romance of an outlaw couple on the run, narrated by a young girl along for the ride. Once again, Malick depicts violence in an understated way that went against the grain of the past decade in American cinema. Another magnificently photographed fire sequence—this time near the end rather than early on—provides the dramatic climax to a series of solipsistic "adventures" suggesting the expulsion from Eden. Other stylistic points of reference were apparent: the carefully composed landscapes shot during the "magic hour," often employing a telephoto lens; the microscopic close-ups of plants and insects; the emphatic contributions of the musical score; and the haunting, original quality of the voiceover narration. Certain parallel scenes—particularly the male protagonist's wanderings through the rich man's mansion and the girl narrator's absorption in viewing a series of pictures, here an illustrated book of jungle creatures—also serve as signature moments.

Voiceover Narration: Linda and Huck Finn

Foremost among these repeated elements is the narrating voice of the girl, unnamed in the diegesis but commonly identified as Linda, following the screenplay and the closing credits. Her commentary, usually related to events as they happen but occasionally digressive ("I've been thinking what to do with my future"), has an intensity and intelligence completely lacking in Holly's account. Although some early reviewers found Malick's technique repetitive, Linda's narration remains spontaneous rather than scripted, sensitive rather than benumbed, "a rich combination of innocence, received wisdom, and weltschmerz" (Zucker 7). While many of the girl's observations possess a vernacular poetry on the page, the voiceover ultimately owes its engaging effect to Linda Manz's uncanny recitation, her urban accent and breathless sincerity sharply contrasting with Holly's enervated country drawl. Both narrations can be described as hypnotic, although in quite different ways: Holly's lulls you into a kind of moral torpor; Linda's stimulates you to imaginative and aesthetic alertness.

If Holly's narrating persona can be compared to Tom Sawyer, eager to please and therefore fundamentally conventional, then Linda's preternatural sensitivity can be likened to that of Huckleberry Finn. Compare, for example, Linda's portrayal of her first experience on a boat with Huck Finn's descriptions of life on the river:

> The sun looks ghostly when there's a mist on the river and everything's quiet. I never knowed it before. You could see people on the shore, but it was far off and you couldn't see what they were doin'. They were probably callin' for help or somethin', or they were tryin' to bury somebody or somethin'.
>
> We seen trees that the leaves are shakin' and it looks like shadows of guys comin' at you and stuff. We heard owl squawkin' away, oonin' away. Some sights that I saw was really spooky that it gave me goose pimples. I felt like old hands touchin' the back of my neck and—and it could be the dead comin' for me or somethin'. (*Days of Heaven*)

The sky looks ever so deep when you lay down on your back in the moonshine; I never knowed it before. And how far a body can hear on the water such nights! (*Adventures of Huckleberry Finn*, chapter 8)

Once there was a thick fog, and the rafts and things that went by was beating tin pans so the steamboats wouldn't run over them. A scow or a raft went by so close we could hear them talking and cussing and laughing—heard them plain; but we couldn't see no sign of them; it made you feel crawly, it was like spirits carrying on that way in the air. (*Adventures of Huckleberry Finn*, chapter 19)

The run-on sentences reflect a child's inability to subordinate experiences at the same time that they help re-create the dynamism of both scenes—everything is changing before the narrator's eyes and ears. The ungrammatical constructions confirm the youngsters' lack of formal education while they add to the authenticity and spontaneity of their descriptions. Elsewhere in the novel, of course, Huck continually employs the onomatopoeia that marks Linda's narration here and feels the same morbid sense of isolation (missing in these passages because Jim is with him). Linda's monologue in this sequence begins with her observation, "Nobody's perfect. There was never a perfect person around. You just got half devil and half angel in you," a moral perspective that echoes the dualistic theology Huck absorbs from Jim: "Dey's two angels hoverin' roun' 'bout him. One uv 'em is white en shiny, en 'tother one is black. De white one gits him to go right, a little while, den de black one sail in en bust it all up" (chapter 4).

Linda's frequent reversion to the second person ("You could see people on the shore") is also a common feature of Huck's narration ("If you think it ain't dismal and lonesome out in a fog that way, by yourself, in the night, you try it once—you'll see" [chapter 15]), with the effect (so different from *Badlands*) of drawing the audience into the scene, creating a bond with the storyteller. Like Huck's, her journey conveys urgency and requires adaptability; their wanderings hardly constitute "adventures," as she first describes them (and as Holly had tried to characterize her interlude in the wilderness), but rather quests for stability and constant learning experiences ("I never knowed it before," Huck and Linda both say). In addition to feelings of insecurity and an acute sensitivity to nature (she imagines herself becoming "a mud doctor, checkin' out the earth underneath"), Linda shares with Huck a fundamental compassion for others. Thus, she empathizes with her newfound friend, the "makin's" girl, when she detects a scar on her ear or when successive boyfriends abandon her, and with the plight of her brother and adoptive sister. Her monologue about the Farmer's fate, remarkably rendered by Manz, manages to transform sentimental images into a deeply moving expression of human connection: "Wasn't no harm in him. You'd give him a flower, he'd keep it forever. He was headed for the boneyard any minute. But he wasn't really goin' around squawkin' about it like some people. In one way, I felt sorry for him, 'cause he had nobody to stand out for him, be by his side, hold his hand when he needs attention or somethin'. That's touchin'." Moreover, Linda's compassion, like Huck's, is not simply "innocent"; she has become aware at an early age of human cruelty and social injustice. She wonders, for example, about the deference paid to the Farmer because of his wealth ("This farmer, he had a big spread and a lot of money. Whoever was sitting in the chair when he'd come around, why did they stand up and give it to him?"). In a similar vein, she defends her brother's immoral scheme to inherit the Farmer's land: "He was tired of livin' like the rest of 'em, nosin' around like a pig in the gutter. He figured some people need more than they got, other people got more than they need. Just a matter of

gettin' us all together." Linda, of course, is no more a communist than Huck is a "low down Abolitionist," but both good-hearted souls respond instinctively to suffering when they confront it.

In the end, both Huck and Linda seem resolved to "light out" again, in the girl's case, to run away from the confines of her new boarding school. In one final voiceover, heard over the beautifully composed long shot of railroad tracks extending to a vanishing point at the break of dawn, Linda expresses best wishes for her acquaintance, imagined as a longtime companion: "This girl, she didn't know where she was goin' or what she was goin' to do. She didn't have no money on her or anything. Maybe she would meet up with a character. I was hopin' things would work out for her. She was a good friend of mine."

History and Myth

The opening credit sequence, with its montage of historical photographs, immediately establishes *Days of Heaven* as a period piece, but Malick treats the past with vacillating verisimilitude. A single image, the well-known picture of President Woodrow Wilson tipping his top hat to acknowledge a crowd, sets the story within a narrow time frame, while one quick close-up of the Amarillo Dispatch within the diegesis specifically dates Wilson's train ride through the Farmer's property as October 7, 1916, although few viewers will be able to read the type. The film thus roots its narrative in a particular moment of the country's history, one rarely treated in earlier American movies (Elia Kazan's *East of Eden* [1955] being a notable exception), but the *treatment* of the period evokes several different eras preceding and following 1916. Many of the initial prologue images depict Ellis Island and urban immigrant street scenes associated with the first decade of the twentieth century. The plot, however, centers on the plight of rural migrant workers in the Texas Panhandle, evoking memories of the Depression, Walker Evans's photographs in *Let Us Now Praise Famous Men* (1939), and John Steinbeck's *The Grapes of Wrath* (1939). In the context of 1978, the closing scenes of American doughboys marching off to war inevitably conjured the fate of soldiers in Vietnam. In representing an American past in each of his features to date, Malick aspires to have it both ways: to re-create the architecture, machinery, furnishings, and costumes of a definitive moment but also to relate those details to the more enduring and resonant qualities of epic and myth.

The mythic dimensions of *Days of Heaven* go well beyond its evocation of Jefferson's agrarianism, Emerson's transcendentalism, Horace Greeley's western migration, or Horatio Alger's rags-to-riches tale. The title derives from Deuteronomy 11:21 ("That your days may be multiplied, and the days of your children, in the land which the Lord swore unto your fathers to give them, as the days of heaven upon the earth"), and other biblical references abound. The plot at times alludes to Genesis, Exodus, and Ruth; the jeremiad Linda relates early on in the film is realized in the apocalyptic fire that follows a plague of locusts.

> I met this guy named Ding-Dong. He told me the whole earth is goin' up in flame. Flames will come out of here and there and they'll just rise up. The mountains are gonna go up in big flames, the water's gonna rise in flames.
>
> There's gonna be creatures runnin' every which way, some of them burnt, half of their wings burnin'. People gonna be screamin' and hollerin' for help. See, the people that have been good—they're gonna go to heaven and escape all the fire. But if you've been bad, God don't even hear you. He don't even hear you talkin'.

From this monologue forward, *Days of Heaven* proceeds with a dark fatality reminiscent of Greek drama as well as biblical prophesy. The film's title first suggests the tenuousness and brevity of human happiness; the ranch foreman's relentless pursuit of Bill, which culminates in the posse's hunting him down in the river, suggests the classical Furies.

Like every Malick film, *Days of Heaven* gives special prominence to the elemental images of earth, air, fire, and water. Seen from the perspective of the film's mythopoetic intentions, such apparently gratuitous shots as the time-lapse micro-close-up of germinating wheat or the ominous low-angle silhouette of the Farmer and his rooftop wind generator can be understood as tonal figures within an epic design rather than simply "artsy" intercuts. The long takes of amber waves of grain billowing in the wind simultaneously evoke the national story and more universal connotations: nature, the good earth, paradise. Similarly, the deus ex machina flying circus, which serves as comic relief from the impending personal tragedy and, with the planes' insignia of the British and German air forces, as a historical marker of the gathering global conflict, connects with earlier images of birds in flight and cerulean skyscapes. The climactic conflagration, the uncontrollable flames consuming the breadth of the widescreen, fulfills the destructive potential of the ominous bonfire dance at harvest time immediately after Abby accepts the Farmer's proposal to stay. In a parallel manner, the dramatic filming of Bill's death in the river harkens back to previous lyrical scenes of the Whitmanesque workers swimming and bathing in a broad stream on the property as well as the furtive couple's midnight tryst, which concludes with a startling underwater shot of Bill's carelessly dropped wine glass.

Another way in which the film achieves mythic proportions is through Malick's often maligned construction of character, his apparent preference for physical typology at the expense of psychological depth. *Days of Heaven* remains his most daring movie in this regard, risking that the director can create something like a modern epic without involving his audience in the personal lives of his characters. Although the reviews and critical articles that followed continually identify the protagonists by name—Bill, Abby, Linda, and occasionally (as in Petric's lengthy review) even "Chuck," the Farmer's name in the original screenplay—a first-time viewer is unlikely to recall any of these for the simple reason that only Bill is identified by name in the diegesis (in Linda's monosyllabic answer to her friend's question about her brother's name). The credits alone make it possible to refer to the film's nontraditional family; the Farmer and Fore-

man, along with all the other workers, remain anonymous. Given Richard Gere's and Brooke Adams's rather one-dimensional performances and Sam Shepard's effective but taciturn presence, the principal players in Malick's classical drama consistently come across as representatives rather than individuals, "undermotivated ciphers" (Donougho 17) for many of the film's critics. But "representatives" *of what?* In literature, this device of limited characterization most often serves the function of allegory, to illustrate a predetermined theme or moral, but Malick seems unconcerned with making his meaning clear. For him, the autonomous presence of the images on the screen, their mute testimony to their own physical existence, remains sufficient.

Visual and Aural Poetics

As "Malick's vision of history and geography is poetic rather than factual" (Petric 40), so too his sense of narrative is lyrical rather than linear. Nothing sets him apart from his contemporaries, not to mention the succeeding generation of American directors, as much as his commitment to cinematic beauty. Almendros has acknowledged Malick's "exceptional knowledge of painting" (234), a compliment that has proven a mixed blessing for critics who liken watching one of his films to touring an art gallery. Many reviewers have noted this film's allusions to Andrew Wyeth (*Christina's World*) and Edward Hopper (*House by the Railroad*). Almendros compares Malick's use of light through side windows to Jan Vermeer's technique in his interiors (235). Many of the group scenes, particularly the harvest celebration, recall Pieter Breughel the Elder. But the visual splendor of these compositions should not detract from the cinematic effects of the almost contantly moving camera (*Days of Heaven* was the first film to employ Panaglide, a prototype of the Steadicam), the carefully choreographed movements within the frame (as in the long shots of harvesting), the several striking montage sequences (beginning with the credits and culminating with the lost war against the insects), and the slow dissolves that signify paradoxically both transition and a dreamy timelessness.

No better example of Malick's aesthetic sensibility can be found than the telephoto long shot of the migrants' train crossing an elevated trestle in the first five minutes of *Days of Heaven*. It is the film's signature shot, just as the billboard (which it schematically resembles) is the signature shot of *Badlands*. The frame is perfectly balanced, with the bridge bisecting earth and sky, the camera subtly panning to keep the horizontally moving train (right to left, to suggest the movement westward) precisely centered. The silhouette gives the image a universal aspect—no distinguishing details or individual riders can be discerned (although the next shot, from a high angle, shows the workers sitting on top of boxcars). The dissipating black smoke, the pale blue sky with puffy clouds, the lofty height of the trestle, and the musical accompaniment of Leo Kottke's "Enderlin" all contribute to the formal design, the magical realism of the image. Its portrait of suspended animation may recall H. H. Bennett's photograph *Leap across the Chasm*, just observed in the opening credit sequence. Both scenes depict a moment of perilous passage and human vulnerability, occluded by the cameraman's intervention.

Days of Heaven proceeds according to this associational structure, building on the visual poetics established in *Badlands*. The narrative begins and ends with similar shots of receding railroad tracks, and trains reappear intermittently carrying seasonal workers, President Wilson, and young soldiers. Malick depicts four kinds of dance—the impromptu breakdown-and-shuffle Linda engages in with the black man, the communal folk dance at harvest time, the belly dance, and Abby's ballet performances, reprised in the epilogue—as another organizational motif. The close-up of the factory furnace in the opening scene is repeated in the view of the giant threshing machine, both images leading to the

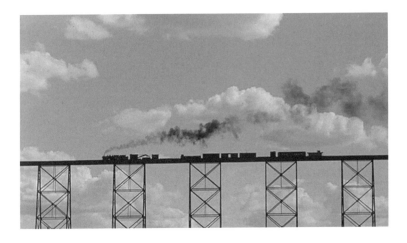

Executive Producer
JACOB BRACKMAN

harvest bonfire and the conflagration at the climax. Linda's strange rec-
ollection of Ding-Dong is echoed in her monologue about Black Jack
during her anxious flight on the boat, where she witnesses small camp
fires by the riverside: "I remember this guy, his name was Black Jack.
He died. He only had one leg, and he died. And I think that was Black
Jack makin' those noises." The white boat itself is an incarnation of the
design the farmer had displayed for Abby made of whitewashed rocks
arranged in an open field.

Beyond creating visual and auditory rhymes that help to mark the
progress of the tale, Malick employs some carefully composed images
for their symbolic value as well as their formal beauty. The still life of
two wine glasses and decanter on a side table, for example, signifies for
Bill, who has moved into the mansion during the couple's honeymoon,
the loss of his lover, whose good fortune he now can only contemplate.
When the wine glasses return in his nocturnal rendezvous with Abby,
Malick concludes the scene with a remarkable underwater close-up of
the glass Bill has broken, as a fish glides around its surface. The image
is mysterious, beautiful, and also ominous, reflecting the recklessness
of this stolen hour. Its symbolic significance becomes manifest in the
equally unexpected underwater shot of Bill's body breaking the surface
of the river in his final moment, the brief cut to slow motion and silence compounding the tragic effect. Only in this culminating figure of

a complex cinematic design does the significance of the initial still life become fully realized, as in metaphysical poetry, a metaphor turned into a conceit.

Other emblems of the film's dark fatality abound: the cutaway to a scarecrow at sunset, the low-angle shots of the whining wind generator, the tracking shots of the monstrous harvesters. Malick precipitates the plague of locusts with an uncanny bird's-eye shot of Linda in the kitchen, a textbook example of how this rarely employed angle (absent almost entirely elsewhere in the director's work) suggests the omniscience of a distant, godlike consciousness overseeing the blind strivings of human beings.

In his foreword to the enlarged edition of *The World Viewed*, Stanley Cavell directly confronts the persistent question of what function Malick's preoccupation with such self-contained "extremities of beauty" in *Days of Heaven* might serve. He attributes the "formal radiance" of these compositions to Heidegger's concept (in *What Is Called Thinking?*) of the "Being of beings," rendered by the artist in the relation of an object or being to its (Platonic) idea. Malick manages this metaphysical feat of representation by acknowledging "a fundamental fact of film's photographic basis: that objects participate in the photographic presence of themselves. Objects projected on a screen are inherently reflexive, they occur as self-referential, reflecting upon their physical origins. Their presence refers to their absence, their location in another place" (xvi). Cavell's analysis may help to explain the spectral quality of the billboard shot in *Badlands*, its multiple evocations of a primordial elsewhere (an unmapped space outside of town, a perfectly ordered domestic space, a lost America) made present in addition to its self-reflexive gesture. It may also explain the otherwise mismatched cut in *Days of Heaven* from Bill standing alone in the vast wheat field to a close-up of a buffalo apparently in close proximity. The incongruous appearance of this perfectly centered image, confirmed by the subsequent long shot of a tranquil buffalo herd, suggests the ideal vision of a past (even in 1916) made immediately present and "participating" in its own being-ness. Cavell's paradigms of presence of absence and self-reflexivity coalesce in the magnificent credit sequence that begins *Days of Heaven*.

The Credit Sequence

Malick's construction of the credit sequence—a montage of twenty-four sepia-toned historical photographs scrutinized with a restless camera, linked by dissolves, and accompanied by Camille Saint-Saëns's orchestral music of the period, the "Aquarium" section from *Carnival of the Animals* (1886)—provides both a cinematic tour de force and an outline of the narrative to follow. The content of the photographs introduces not only the film's time period but its "argument," understood in the old-fashioned sense of the outline of its plot.

The opening still, a long view of a crowded city avenue, becomes a kind of establishing shot for a series of urban portraits, including Lewis Hine's famous photograph of boys playing stickball in a tenement alley, a pastime that will later be reenacted on the farm, and the equally familiar *Power House Mechanic Working on Steam Pump*, which stands in for Bill's brutal work in the steel mill. The first thirteen images all depict city life, with Wilson (number eight) being the only recognizable historical figure and thereby dating the period. There is a close-up of a veiled bride and a group portrait of young girls in conversation, scenes that also will prove to be parts of the story to come. The twelfth picture, workers congregating around a storefront advertising construction jobs at three dollars a day, becomes noteworthy when, not long after, we see the ranch foreman hiring sackers for exactly the same pay.

These scenes shift away from the big city with the picture of a couple of streetcars on a muddy street (number fourteen), soon followed by H. H. Bennett's photograph of two men in a rowboat in the Wisconsin Dells and a stirring portrait of a young woman in a white sailor dress sitting on a rock gazing out to sea. These images, combined with Bennett's *Leap across the Chasm,* suggest by prolepsis the couple's honeymoon and the heavenly days between harvests. The montage then returns to tenement life. The penultimate photograph, a slightly furtive man and woman walking on boards to enter a building, looks very much like the town in the film's closing sequence, while the final image of boys on a slag heap leads the spectator into the diegesis—but not before the twenty-fifth still shot, Linda Manz sitting forlornly on city cobblestones. This portrait of a fictional character whose voice will now begin narrating serves as a perfect example of "the Kuleshov effect," the hallmark of Soviet montage theory whereby the editing process creates a signification by association with previous images: in this case, the photograph of a young woman taken in 1978 is understood as another in a series of street urchins living around the turn of the century, her otherwise blank expression interpreted as reflecting the impact of urban poverty.

Although Saint-Saëns's "Aquarium" theme has so frequently reappeared in television commercials and movies that it has become a musical cliché, its deployment over the credits remains original and particularly appropriate. The melody recalls music dimly remembered from childhood, reflecting the imaginative sensibility of the narrator, evoking nostalgia in the audience, and transforming the connotations of the stills. As Richard Power has suggested, the music "casts a romantic glow on these particular images, while its associations with the social and leisure qualities of classical music contrast with the poverty and labour depicted in the photographs" (103). The glissando musically imitates the smooth tracking, panning, and zoom movements of the camera, subtly inducing an altered consciousness in the audience at the onset of the mythic tale. The "Aquarium" theme occurs twice more in *Days of Heaven*, approximately at the middle and end—when Wilson's train makes its ghostly appearance and during Linda's dawn escape from boarding school—thereby adding a structural element to its associations with subjectivity. In two specific shots—when Linda gazes at the pages of a book of animals and in the underwater close-up of the fish swimming around Bill's broken wine glass—Malick appears to allude to the title of Saint-Saëns's composition.

Through such obvious directorial interventions (editing, camera movement, nondiegetic music), Malick deliberately subordinates the documentary function of the credit sequence in favor of artistic expressivity. In doing so, he focuses attention on *cinema* rather than photography, on the construction of the past rather than its recording. "We are asked to consider film as a vehicle for speculation and contemplation," Carole Zucker argues, "to interrogate the composition and juxtaposition of the film's images, not to abandon ourselves to the specular experience" (4). In response to the sheer virtuosity of Malick's version of a modern cinema of attractions, however, *we do both*. Like the Farmer overseeing the harvest, the film audience regards the ensuing action in comfortable upholstery and at a safe distance, "enjoying the spectacle of the labor of others [both the field workers and the filmmakers] and a landscape so beautiful it is at times hard to care about anything else" (Wondra 13).

Other moments in *Days of Heaven* foreground the process of looking and then constructing meaning: the Farmer peering through his rooftop telescope (with accompanying iris shot), taking photographs on his honeymoon, and observing Bill and Linda's silhouetted pantomime in the gazebo; the views in depth from inside the bunkhouse through the rectangular (widescreen) window; the multiple instances of Bill's voyeuristic gaze at the privileged life inside the mansion. Each of these mediated perspectives subtly underscores how the filmmaker controls what we see—and, perhaps, how the history of cinema (newsreel, the Western) has affected our perception of history. In the most explicit of these self-reflexive techniques, Malick includes a movie within the movie, comparable to the pseudo-newsreel inserted into *Badlands*, when the flying vaudeville troupe projects Chaplin's *The Immigrant* (1917; a minor anachronism given the appearance of Wilson's train in the immediately preceding episode) as part of their private performance. Linda's narrative over the brief clip of the ship's passengers roped together on the rocking deck gives expression to the growing tensions on the farm as it counterpoints Chaplin's comedy: "The Devil just sittin' there laughin'. He's glad when people does bad. Then he sends them to the snake house. He just sits there and laughs and watch, while you're sittin' there all tied up and snakes are eatin' your eyes out. They go down your throat and eat all your systems out." While Chaplin's silent classic provides comic relief, Linda's apocalyptic commentary describes the Devil's attack on "your eyes," thereby imposing the interrogation of the film's images— Malick's film as well as Chaplin's—that Zucker has suggested. Although neither *The Thin Red Line* nor *The New World* is as blatantly self-reflexive as the films of the 1970s, Malick will deploy a more complex voiceover narration in a similar contrapuntal way to call attention to the integrity and autonomy—the "Being of beings"—of his images.

Disillusion and Resiliency

For all its visual and auditory appeal, *Days of Heaven,* more clearly than *Badlands,* indicates its central thematic concern, America's loss of innocence. Malick provides a specific reminder of where the spectator's critical attention should be directed when a shadowy hand intrudes across the screen to point to the Statue of Liberty in Chaplin's film. The American Dream symbolized by that iconic image, broadly understood as the aspiration for a better life and more narrowly defined as the opportunity to own property, profit according to one's labor, and ensure domestic tranquility, is continually questioned in *Days of Heaven*. Each of the adult protagonists endures disappointment and disillusionment: Bill has never made "the big score," Abby has not been rescued from poverty by the attentions of rich men, the Farmer has married a fallen angel. Even Linda's friend, the "makin's" girl, has been spurned by at least two boyfriends. Bill's regret, of course, is the greatest of all; his farewell scene with Abby, in which he acknowledges his mistake ("I got nobody to blame but myself") and releases all claim to her, anticipates Captain Smith's final parlay with Pocahontas in *The New World*. For the men, disillusionment ends in tragedy and death. But *Days of Heaven* ends as something more than an epic tragedy. There remains all that vast natural beauty and the economic promise the land still holds, despite the fiery destruction of the farm. There is also the resiliency of the women and the exhilarating prospect signified by their restless journeys towards a new life. Even Linda's sorrowful companion bounces back from disappointment: "I don't wait two hours for nobody," she declares.

Beyond the personal struggles of the protagonists to realize the American Dream, *Days of Heaven* depicts the devolution of another original national myth, Jefferson's pastoral ideal, famously described in Leo Marx's seminal study *The Machine in the Garden*. The climactic destruction of the crop, along with the women's flight via railroad, may be interpreted as reflecting the triumph of an industrial economy over an agrarian one and the consequent transformation of American culture in the twentieth century. Balancing the romantic landscapes and bucolic interludes, Malick's film is replete with artifacts of the new industrial age: trains, of course, but also cars, trucks, threshers, tractors, planes, motorcycles, adding machines, and movie projectors. Moreover, no moral value attaches to either opposing force: nature can be monstrous, as when the grasshoppers implacably devour the stalks of wheat; machines can be beautiful, as when the harvesters in silhouette billow smoke at the end of day. The film's closing image suggests a synthesis of these contending elements, as the receding railroad tracks meld with the farmland at dawn.

Like all of Malick's films, *Days of Heaven* resists simple moral or ideological judgments. Bill may be a crude schemer with a bad temper, but he does take responsibility for his family and his own failures; Abby may have exploited the Farmer's trust, but she ultimately is moved by love, overcome by guilt, and deepened by affection for Linda. The Farmer, although detached from life by his wealth, remains, in some respects, Bill's lost double, irretrievably separated from him by socioeconomic circumstances: they physically resemble each other (a fortuitous result from the reluctant casting of Gere), share a talent for juggling ("He used to juggle apples," Linda relates in her opening monologue, while Abby shows off her husband's juggling skills in the gazebo), and, like Cain and Abel, seem bound together by a terrible fate, a kind of sickness rather than sin. Abby and Linda also share a common destiny: starting their lives as child laborers, they end as survivors, true sisters. Malick's representation of characters thus apparently aspires to a transcendence of individual identity to be displayed again in his later films.

Although *Days of Heaven* undoubtedly displays the "post-Vietnam, post-Watergate apocalyptic vision" of lost American innocence found in other films of the era (Zucker 2), it does not submit entirely to the same disillusionment as, for example, *Straw Dogs* (1971), *The Godfather, Part II*, or *The Deer Hunter.* Perhaps this thematic ambiguity— using allegorical characters and motifs to illustrate the inadequacy of the allegorical habit of mind—accounts for the tepid response among professional critics. Without knowing it at the time, Malick may have been reaching for the kind of synthetic vision through which Paradise might be regained in the midst of a fallen world that would mark his return to filmmaking more than two decades later.

The Thin Red Line

The Return of the Prodigal Auteur

The announcement of Terrence Malick's return to filmmaking as screenwriter and director of *The Thin Red Line*, based on James Jones's bestselling 1962 novel, created considerable buzz among cineastes, Hollywood professionals, and Internet groupies. The two decades since *Days of Heaven* had produced rare Malick sightings, principally in Paris and Los

Angeles, and reports of several aborted film projects, most prominently the rejected script for the Jerry Lee Lewis biopic and a similarly unfulfilled adaptation of Walker Percy's 1961 novel *The Moviegoer.* In November 1993, the Brooklyn Academy of Music presented a six-week workshop on Malick's play *Sanshô the Bailiff,* a staging of the story upon which Kenji Mizoguchi's classic film is based. It proved to be an unhappy collaboration with the celebrated Polish filmmaker Andrzej Wajda, who directed, and a financial flop for the producers, Malick's fellow Texans Robert Geisler (who had known him for twenty years) and John Roberdeau. Nevertheless, Geisler and Roberdeau persisted in their tireless efforts to engage their artistic hero as director of *The Thin Red Line.* (For a full account of the Geisler/Roberdeau–Malick relationship, see Peter Biskind's lengthy 1998 *Vanity Fair* article.) With the considerable help of Malick's former agent, Michael Medavoy, and after nearly a decade of cajoling, negotiating, and financing (at a personal cost of nearly $1 million), the producers, careless of what they wished for, got their man: Malick signed to write and direct *The Thin Red Line.*

The American film industry as well as the general movie audience had undergone enormous changes during Malick's absence, as a result of multinational corporations acquiring the old studios and the tremendous commercial success of blockbusters like *Jaws* and *Star Wars.* High-concept productions with established stars and global marketing strategies had all but squeezed out independent, idiosyncratic films like *Badlands* and *Days of Heaven* that could find a coterie audience on the art-house or university circuit. Sony originally was to finance *The Thin Red Line* but abruptly dropped the project, fearing cost overruns on the $52 million project, "moderate by contemporary standards" (Flanagan 129). Prodded by Medavoy and another experienced producer, George Stevens Jr. (who had invested in *Badlands*), Fox 2000 took over the picture on condition that several recognizable stars play the leading roles, which overturned Malick's original conception. The director's artistic reputation still loomed so large, however, that a virtual "feeding frenzy" (Biskind, "Runaway" 217) of actors interested in working with him offered their services. The truly astonishing list of performers reported to have done screen tests or private readings for the film—or to have had their work left on the cutting-room floor—includes Martin Sheen,

Dermot Mulroney, Kevin Costner, Billy Bob Thornton, Bill Pullman, Lukas Haas, Viggo Mortensen, and Mickey Rourke. Although names like Sean Penn, Nick Nolte, John Travolta, and George Clooney (the latter two making only cameo appearances) figured prominently in Fox's promotion, the real star of the film's advertising campaign was undoubtedly Terrence Malick himself, the prodigal auteur.

Despite understandable fears about the director's ability to complete the project, *The Thin Red Line* came in on time and at budget, although certainly not without complications along the way. The production took a hundred days, with most of the shooting in Australia and the Solomon Islands (which include Guadalcanal, site of the costliest battle in the Pacific Theater and the setting for Jones's novel), during which time Malick frequently quarreled with his longtime backers Geisler and Roberdeau, ultimately banning them from the set and threatening to remove their names from the credits. The cinematographer John Toll, an all-star himself who had won an Academy Award for *Dances with Wolves* (1990), initially fretted about Malick's lack of technical expertise, relentless shooting schedule (the raw cut exceeded a million feet, nearly six hours), and improvisational methods (Pizzello 45, 56, 46). The editing process, which involved cutting the running time by more than half as well as adding the voiceovers that were never part of the shooting script, proved excruciating (again) for Malick, not to mention frustrating for numerous actors and the film's composer, Hans Zimmer. But perhaps the biggest obstacle facing the completed picture was competition from Steven Spielberg's hugely successful World War II epic, *Saving Private Ryan*, released only two months before *The Thin Red Line.*

Spielberg, of course, had become (with George Lucas) the supreme purveyor of American commercial moviemaking since *Jaws*. After a string of nearly uninterrupted hits (including *Close Encounters of the Third Kind, E.T.,* the Indiana Jones franchise, and *Jurassic Park,* as well as his "prestige" pictures *The Color Purple* and *Schindler's List*), Spielberg in 1998 could be accurately described as "the anti-Malick (in terms of industriousness, public recognition and commercial achievement)" (Flanagan 124), a *brand* as much as a director whose output during the two decades of Malick's hiatus was widely admired and increasingly revered. Compared to Spielberg's craftsmanship, energy, and clear moral tone (even *Schindler's List* provided an uplifting epilogue),

Malick seemed a dour aesthete, almost an anachronism. The antiwar mythos of the 1970s, born from the Vietnam experience, now appeared "inadequate against the revived myth of the global war as the Good War" (Streamas 138), an historical judgment resoundingly confirmed by the publication of Tom Brokaw's bestselling tribute, *The Greatest Generation*, in the same year as *Saving Private Ryan* and *The Thin Red Line*. In the midst of an economic boom and following the implosion of the Soviet Union, America on the brink of the new millennium (and with no intuition of the events of September 11, 2001) had moved beyond the critical introspection and doubt of the Watergate era to a period of renewed national self-confidence and patriotism. In this climate, Malick's film, no matter how eagerly anticipated by connoisseurs of American cinema nostalgically hoping for a revival of New Hollywood's golden hour, hardly had a chance against Spielberg's latest epic.

A brief comparison of two similar scenes at the beginning and end of both films illustrates the directors' contrasting approaches to their common subject. Following the narrative structure ingrained by television drama, *Saving Private Ryan* opens with an intense, explosive action sequence, the American landing at Omaha Beach. After a lyrical prologue that reveals nothing about the impending invasion, *The Thin Red Line* depicts a similarly tense group of GIs running onto the beach at Guadalcanal, followed by . . . nothing. The Japanese are nowhere to be found, and the soldiers meet no resistance as they head into the jungle. As in Herzog's *Aguirre, Wrath of God*, where the conquistadores are continually threatened by unseen natives while surrounded by thick vegetation, unrelenting heat, and the eerie sounds of exotic birds, Malick sustains the tension "simply by having nothing happen" (Doherty 84) amidst the perpetual menace. In a moment reminiscent of Herzog's presentation of the strange native pipe player in *Aguirre*, Malick punctuates the single-file march across the island with the anomalous appearance of an elderly Melanesian man who passes close by the line of soldiers from the opposite direction without exchanging a glance or a word. In the conclusion to *Saving Private Ryan*, Spielberg delivers the film's patriotic message with an elaborate scene at the vast cemetery commemorating the Normandy invasion, including a deft digital morph to connect past and present. Near the end of *The Thin Red Line*, following the sacrificial death of Private Witt, Malick shows the reduced C Company marching past a small makeshift graveyard on the island, the white crosses already less a military memorial than a part of the landscape. In both scenes, then, where Spielberg opts for thematic clarity, Malick aspires to, if not ambiguity, at most suggestiveness, and where Spielberg's style throughout *Saving Private Ryan* is consistently journalistic, Malick's in *The Thin Red Line* alternates between graphic realism and cinematic poetry.

With Spielberg's popular take on the war movie in mind, reviewers of *The Thin Red Line* ranged from enthusiastic to befuddled to decidedly disappointed. Many critics were skeptical of Malick's "maudlin metaphysics," which seemed to lapse into an "inexcusable descent into the sentimental" without the leavening effect of irony so evident in his first two films (Whalen 162). The negative commentaries seized on the platitudinous or pretentious quality of the film's voiceovers ("like what Hemingway might have come up with if he wrote fortune cookies" [Taylor]), the signature element of *Badlands* and *Days of Heaven,* as a measure of Malick's failure this time. In a particularly nasty essay published in *Salon* entitled "The Big Dead One," Charles Taylor dared to say what more respectful writers left between the lines, calling the film a "self-indulgent throwback to the '70s" and indicting the director for wanting audiences "to react not to the story or the characters, but to his artistry." Others, of course, wrote not to bury Malick but to praise him. Several respected voices, led by J. Hoberman in *The Village Voice,* championed the film's ambition, originality, and visual beauty but invariably with qualifications that acknowledged, in Hoberman's striking phrase, "the movie's brave, strange, eroded nobility" (Hoberman, "Wars Within" 117). Judging by the scholarly articles and Internet blogs that have followed, ambivalence about the film's ultimate value has persisted.

The equivocal response to *The Thin Red Line* generally centers on four main reservations: 1) the historical inaccuracies and departures from Jones's novel; 2) the lack of dramatic structure; 3) the unresolved philosophical musings conveyed primarily through voiceovers; 4) the misuse of star actors, principally as a result of drastic editing. It might prove useful at the outset of this analysis to suggest how these "problems" help to define Malick's particular kind of filmmaking. *The Thin Red Line* adheres to the principles of verisimilitude and historical representation more stringently than either *Badlands* or *Days of Heaven.* The factual errors that have been noted—the most significant being that very few Japanese prisoners were captured on Guadalcanal (as noted in Jones's novel)—remain essentially trivial. On the other hand, many reviewers (Roger Ebert and Stuart Klawans chief among them) and later scholars have complained about Malick's departures from his literary source. Yet Biskind reports that the director "agonized about every deviation from Jones's novel, no matter how trivial" ("Runaway" 210), going so far as to seek the author's widow's approval for any changes. All evidence suggests that Malick's intention, as in *The New World*, was to reconstruct the conditions of an historical event as experienced and then described by someone (Jones here, John Smith in the next film) who actually lived through it.

The absence of a character-driven plot with the usual goal-oriented narrative trajectory of classical Hollywood cinema (of which *Saving Private Ryan* may stand as a paradigm) can be traced to Malick's conception of war as a chaotic series of spasmodic conflicts surrounded by long interludes of tension, boredom, debauchery, and thought. In this respect (minus the debauchery), along with his attention to the natural world and interest in characters as human types, Malick follows the style and themes of the first classic American war novel, Stephen Crane's *The Red Badge of Courage*, written almost exactly a century earlier. In its contemplation of existential questions and its interrogation of nature's beauty and indifference to man's fate, Crane's novel, as much as Jones's, remains the (unacknowledged) inspiration for *The Thin Red Line*. Indeed, its closing passage reflects, remarkably, the ordinary soldier's yearning for transcendence, his aspiration for the "other world" Private Witt appears to attain in his final moments: "He had rid himself of the red sickness of battle. The sultry nightmare was in the past. He had been an animal blistered and sweating in the heat and pain of war. He turned now with a lover's thirst to images of tranquil skies, fresh meadows, cool brooks—an existence of soft and eternal peace. Over the river a golden ray of sun came through the hosts of leaden rain clouds" (*The Red Badge of Courage*). Even Crane's characteristic color imagery, evident here in his phrase "the red sickness of battle," seems to reverberate in Malick's mantra at the time to describe his film's core idea, "the green poison" of war (Biskind, "Runaway" 210).

The Thin Red Line's multiple voiceovers are problematic for several reasons: their abstract reflections and philosophical concerns seem at odds with the gritty circumstances of the soldiers at war and lead to no definitive conclusions; with the exception of Bell's obsession with his wife's love, they do not readily correspond to Jones's original characterizations; the voices themselves are difficult to distinguish from each other, blurring individual identity in a polyphonic chorus; the questions themselves and the language employed often seem sophomoric and trite. The late decision to use offscreen commentary and to employ many voices instead of a single narrator, as in the first two films, probably reflects Malick's effort to adapt Jones's technique of omniscient point of view as the author continuously shifts the novel's narrative consciousness among more than twenty members of C for Charlie Company. The similarity in the timbre of the voices themselves—Witt and Bell speak with southern accents that make them difficult to tell apart—conveys the collective identity of the company (and, indeed, of all soldiers, all men) and raises the pervasive Emersonian theme of "one big soul that everyone's a part of" that Witt first enunciates early in the film and that culminates in the final voiceover about "the workings of one mind, the features of the same face." That the questions lead to no certain answers should surprise neither the philosophically trained (particularly those familiar with Heidegger, who argued for the significance of confusion) nor audiences familiar with the director's prior work; that their expression comes in trite formulations is appropriate to the education of the minds that conceive them. Indeed, as one reviewer acknowledged, "They claim a measure of their pathos from their forthright platitude" (Morrison 38).

Malick's handling of his prestigious cast, particularly as concerns editing decisions, ultimately serves to foreground the anonymity and expendability of the wartime soldier. The only true "star" turns—performances where the actor's established persona is readily recognizable—belong to the commanding officers outside of C Company, Brigadier General Quintard (John Travolta) and Colonel Tall (Nick Nolte). Sean Penn's Welsh is certainly a strong performance, but his character is absent for long periods and deliberately blends in with the rest of the company in the background of many shots. Two other important roles, Privates Bell and Witt, seem to have been cast because of Ben Chaplin's and James Caviezel's resemblance to one another, a visual affinity compounded by their meditative speech. Another major actor, John Cusack, first appears halfway through the film and, after his heroic action leading an attack on the Japanese bunker, is seen no more. George Clooney, already a box-office star, appears for less than a minute as the replacement for the company's deposed captain (the far less familiar Elias Koteas). Beyond the practical necessity of leaving behind many worthy scenes in the editing room, Malick's treatment of his A-list actors serves to underscore how the military institution strips away individual identity but also how war can confirm what Stephen Crane defined as "the subtle brotherhood of men" ("The Open Boat") and what James Jones, describing Witt, called "an almost sexual ecstasy of comradeship" (319).

The "Malick" Film and the War Movie

The Thin Red Line's rapturous images of nature, conspicuous use of voiceover, and "aestheticist detachment" (Morrison 35) naturally provoke comparisons to Malick's films of the 1970s. Once again, he subordinates historical markers of the narrative—there are no cultural references to date the period, no ideological statements about the American cause in World War II, and barely a mention of the strategic importance of Guadalcanal or the particular battle for Hill 210—to its mythic dimensions: the exile from Eden, the carnage of war, the yearning for transcendence. Certain signature images return: shafts of light through the trees, exotic animals, birdcages, rivers, fires. The musical score, Zimmer's Oscar-nominated New Age sound track, once more figures prominently. But these same elements that won the director critical acclaim for his first two pictures—the high seriousness in resistance to his hip contemporaries and the tradition of classical Hollywood melodrama—now seemed slightly stodgy in an era defined by epic blockbusters like *Braveheart* (1995) and *Titanic* (1997) and the postmodernist glibness of Quentin Tarantino and the Coen brothers.

Malick's persistent outsider status in relation to established industry practices and even the counterstrategies of independent filmmakers can be illustrated by *The Thin Red Line*'s transformation of the combat movie. Beyond its obvious contrasts with *Saving Private Ryan,* the film differs from nearly every other significant example of the genre. It has "none of the post-adolescent bombast of Francis Ford Coppola's *Apocalypse Now* (1979), the cloying self-righteousness of Oliver Stone's *Platoon* (1986), or the gnawing, sentimental nationalism of *Saving Private Ryan* (1998)" (Critchley). It also lacks the cynicism and despair of Kubrick's *Full Metal Jacket* (1987), a film with which it is, surprisingly, rarely compared. The battle sequences, although intense and brutal, hardly contribute to a sense of the film's plot or the significance of the American victory. As in his earlier pictures, Malick treats violence as idiomatic rather than possessing a special meaning beyond wasteful destructiveness. "That violence is unequivocally presented as evil, and, extraordinary for a so-called war film (especially one about World War II), there is not a single expression of patriotic sentiment in the film and there is no attempt whatsoever to provide a moral or historical justification or even explanation for the violence of war" (Bersani and Dutoit 129) sets *The Thin Red Line* apart from its predecessors within the genre. "Malick's Guadalcanal diary [the title of one of Hollywood's best movies about the Pacific campaign] is more a meditation on nature," Thomas Doherty has observed, "than an evocation of war" (83).

Unlike the typical Hollywood World War II combat film (including the 1964 version of Jones's novel) or its post-Vietnam successors, *The Thin Red Line* does not dwell on relationships within the company, usually depicted in American movies as a melting pot of readily recognizable ethnic types. (With this distinction in mind, Malick's decision to change Jones's C Company captain from the Jewish Stein to the Greek Staros seems calculated to avoid any stereotyping that might undermine his more universal concerns or his cast of soldiers as "all faces of the same man." Thus, both Staros and his commander and antagonist, Colonel Tall, find occasion to speak in Greek.) Paradoxically, Malick manages to bring forth the familiar idea of camaraderie and the more transcendentalist thought about "one big soul" by swiftly moving among a troop of largely undifferentiated GIs who are rarely seen actually interacting. Michel Chion has noted the general absence of communal ceremonies and how, during collective scenes like mail call or the attack on the enemy bivouac following the firefight, "the sound of the group is muffled, dampened, heard from afar," as if recalled from the distance of memory or dream (29). Despite the film's length and the number of speaking parts in addition to the voiceovers, very little dialogue is actually *exchanged,* and Malick's cutting often separates the speakers. Even in those infrequent moments of personal conflict—Witt versus Welsh, or Staros versus Tall—the men remain civil with one another, their differences ultimately repressed, as in Welsh's mournful riposte at Witt's graveside, "Where's your spark now?" or Tall's dismissal of

Staros: "It's not necessary for you to ever tell me that I'm right. Ever. We'll assume it."

In addition to the authoritarian Colonel Tall's gung-ho thirst for military victory spurred by his own demonic ambition, the jungle topography, hidden Asian enemy, burning straw villages, and chaotic combat sequences all reflect the film's vision of World War II through a Vietnam War mindscreen rather than, as Colin McCabe has claimed, an effort to forget Vietnam (12). Although they represent opposing philosophies, Welsh's existentialist skepticism and Witt's transcendentalist idealism share a fundamental alienation from the military establishment, clearly signified by the private's extended AWOL sojourn at the beginning of the film (expanded from a single parenthetical phrase in Jones's novel [106]), but also by Witt's ideological protest: "It's all about property!" Even Private Bell's romantic flashbacks to several sensual encounters with his wife as well as his plaintive appeals to their union ("Be with me now") resonate with the Vietnam era's faith that "all you need is love." The fact that she betrays him in the end (as in the novel) contrasts sharply with Captain Miller's (Tom Hanks) fulfilled hope of returning home to domestic bliss in *Saving Private Ryan* but does not nullify the value of Bell's dream, which helps keep him alive and remains vivid testimony to his imagination.

Despite the resonating Vietnam experience, *The Thin Red Line* cannot be readily categorized as an antiwar film. For one thing, it is simply too beautiful; for another, it reveals much wider concerns. Rather like Walt Whitman's poignant Civil War poems (which never depict scenes of battle), Malick's film, no less than his central trio of combat soldiers (Witt, Welsh, and Bell) aspires to, if not redemption, reconciliation.

> Word over all, beautiful as the sky,
> Beautiful that war and all its deeds or carnage must in time be utterly
>   lost,
> That the hands of the sisters Death and Night incessantly softly wash
>   again, and ever again, this soil'd world.
>   (Whitman, "Reconciliation," from *Drum-Taps*)

No wonder, then, that audiences raised on such post-Vietnam "prestige" war films as *Apocalypse Now, Full Metal Jacket, Platoon,* and *Saving Private Ryan,* not to mention *Rambo: First Blood* (1982) and its sequels, might be confused by Malick's take on the genre.

Adapting James Jones's Novel

Considering the director's apparent intention to remain true to a novel he much admired as well as the film's direct reproduction of Jones's dialogue and oblique references to many incidental episodes, *The Thin Red Line* seems to have inverted the standard formula for "faithful" adaptation of literature into film: it generally adheres to the *plot* but violates the prevailing *spirit* of Jones's work. It is astonishing, in fact, to realize how much detail from a five-hundred-page novel Malick has managed to incorporate. His reverence for the story, however, sometimes leads to undeveloped, cryptic, or anomalous moments. For example, the brief view of a soldier (PFC Doll) on the landing vessel stealing another GI's pistol corresponds to an extended episode in the first chapter of the novel, but without its attendant consequences. Similarly, the scene late in the film in which the new company commander, Captain Bosche (Clooney), addresses his men serves no apparent dramatic purpose other than to recite his speech from the novel about "family." His reference to the "swipe" (homemade liquor the men consume in drunken revelry after the battle) makes little or no sense within the movie. Neither does Witt's parlay with the wounded soldier who declines his offer to help him back to camp, an incident elaborated in the novel, tell us much about either man's character or the circumstances of war. And while Jones spends considerable attention on the individual animosities among the men—in particular, Corporal Fife's cruel fistfight with Private Weld and Private Mazzi's insubordinate verbal attack on Lieutenant Band—Malick includes only glimpses of men grappling during the bivouac, images that seem unmotivated and contradictory to the film's humanist theme.

Of course, the director does impose a few substantial changes from the novel. The film's opening three sequences—Witt and another un-identified soldier AWOL among the island natives, Witt and Welsh's dialogue in the brig, Tall and Quintard's conversation aboard the destroy-er—are (save for that parenthetical phrase about "property") entirely Malick's invention. Two of the film's central characters are substantially changed from the novel, where Witt, rather than a beatific idealist, is a bigoted eccentric ("Witt who hated niggers because they all wanted to vote. From beneath the shell, in shadow, his hard implacable eyes peered out like the eyes of some ferretlike animal" [442]) and Welsh, rather than embodying a Bogart-like integrity, totters on the brink of insanity ("There were times, moments, when Welsh realized that he was quite mad" [424]). Witt does not die a sacrificial hero in the novel; the film excises Jones's frequent descriptions of homosexual feelings and acts or particularly gruesome images like the company's discovery of the mutilated and beheaded GI (156) or the evidence of Japanese cannibalism (446).

Jones's *The Thin Red Line,* like its companion World War II novel, *From Here to Eternity* (1951), chronicles the experience of battle in graphic detail and language, following the tradition of American literary naturalism in its emphasis on human beings struggling to survive in a world of powerful forces that they cannot control and rarely understand. Like his predecessors in the genre, Stephen Crane, Ernest Hemingway, and Norman Mailer (*The Naked and the Dead,* 1948), Jones emphasizes the physical and psychological responses of the soldiers to combat in a way that contrasts with the sentimental renderings of war in patriotic art. Several passages mock how popular films reconstruct battles to make them exciting and meaningful.

> So Bugger's little attack was over. If this were a movie, this would be the end of the show and something would be decided.
> In a movie or a novel they would dramatize and build to the climax of the attack. When the attack came in the film or novel, it would be satisfying. It would decide something. It would have a semblance of meaning and a semblance of an emotion. And immediately after, it would be over. The audience could go home and think about the semblance of meaning and feel the semblance of the emotion. Even if the hero got killed, it would still make sense. Art, Bell decided, creative art—was shit. (237)

One can imagine Malick underlining this passage, keeping it in mind throughout the shoot. Certainly he adheres to the author's conviction that all war stories—those told by the veterans ("Men changed their wars in the years that followed after they fought them" [381]), but especially those told by the movies—distort the true experience of combat, and so he deliberately eschews normal dramatic structure in his film, imposing a prolonged denouement that does not "decide" anything.

In keeping with the style of literary naturalism, Jones's characters are ordinary, neither heroic nor larger than life, and the author's language is unembellished, occasionally crude in keeping with their ethnicity, education, and experience. Instead of subordination, the sentences in the typical passage cited above employ compounds; the vocabulary remains deliberately limited and repetitive; the vulgar metaphor at the end stands apart as the sole example of figurative language; the thought seems hardly profound. Malick's film strays from the style and spirit of its source by adding elements of romanticism—the pantheistic regard for nature, the persistent quest for moral truth, the lyrical interludes of intensified perception—to the violent scenes of struggle and the pervasiveness of chance that mark Jones's novel. Rather than foregrounding, as Jones does, the physical aspects of the soldiers' lives—Fife's defecating in the field, Bell's sexual arousal in battle, Doll's homoerotic attraction to Arbre—Malick replaces these bodily functions with images of a prelapsarian Paradise or a fallen but still beautiful world. Zimmer's sonorous score, the chorus of native villagers at the beginning and end of the film, and, again, the sheer sound of human voices speaking off-camera words of love, hope, and faith add an auditory complement to the film's aesthetic design. Malick's adaptation of Jones's novel is thus a hybrid, combining a journalistic view of the dark necessity that compels men to war with a poetic expression of the opposite impulse to find beauty in the heart of darkness.

The scholar Jimmie Cain has shown how the film is a hybrid in another sense, an amalgam of the first two novels in Jones's war trilogy (*Whistle,* published posthumously in 1978, is the third). He argues persuasively that Witt is largely based on the character of J. J. Prewitt in *From Here to Eternity* and shows how the three opening sequences missing from *The Thin Red Line* have their sources in Jones's earlier novel. Malick's depiction of Witt, according to Cain, represents "a reincarnated Prewitt in an intermediate stage of soldierly development" (15), motivated by a sense of loyalty to the company and a spiritual dimension that derives from Jones's portrait of Prewitt. The film's Witt, as performed by the actor who would go on to play Jesus in Mel Gibson's *The Passion of the Christ* (2004), has been freed from the bigotry and crudity of Jones's characterization. His truth-seeking and sacrificial death lie at the center of Malick's cinema of the most recent decade, although they run diametrically counter to the novel's determinism. While keeping an eye on Jones's esteemed fiction and the tragic waste that modern war engenders, Malick, no less than his version of the perpetually AWOL Witt, envisions "another world," a cinema of truth and beauty.

This World and the Other World

The film's central philosophical issue, entirely Malick's invention in adapting Jones's novel, hinges on the initial dialogue between Welsh and Witt in the brig:

> WELSH: You'll never be a true soldier. Not in God's world. In this world, a man himself ain't nothing. And there ain't no world but this one.
> WITT: You're wrong, Top. I've seen another world.

Although these two antagonists reach a tenuous detente in their third and final conversation, they remain in fundamentally different worlds. Welsh's is much closer to Jones's deterministic conception of battlefield life: a world of powerful, unseen political and economic forces ("property!") in which conflict is the norm, men are isolated ("in a box"), and survival remains up to chance. Witt's vision of another, ideal world corresponds to the harmonious integration of man and nature he worships during his AWOL sojourn with the island natives, an unfallen Paradise that Melville described in his first novel, *Typee* (1846), and that Pocahontas embodies in *A New World*. It is the mythic Eden of the American Adam, as delineated in R. W. B. Lewis's celebrated study, restored to his natural dignity and freed from the depravity of his forefathers.

Malick displays this world in a signature montage shortly after C Company lands and enters the tropical forest. Initiated by low-angle shots of shafts of light piercing the treetops, followed by a close-up of paired tropical birds, these luminous images give way to the background of a smoking battlefield as the soldiers poised to confront the enemy march up a hill, but a southern-accented voice (that initially seems to be Witt reflecting his pantheistic outlook but turns out to be Bell recalling moments of married love) continues in reverent voiceover: "Who are you, who live in all these many forms? . . . Your glory, mercy, peace, truth. You give calm spirit, courage, the contented heart."

As a hybrid work of art, Malick's film continually repositions itself between these two worlds, real and ideal, and tries to reconcile them

by moving with a restless camera from stark scenes of anxiety and carnage to tranquil moments of contemplation and wholeness. It is a risky, difficult task the director has set for himself, almost as if he were H. H. Bennett capturing his son poised in midair over the chasm in the photograph that seems so suggestive of Malick's ultimate vision. In these last two films in particular, he seems intent on employing the camera to replicate Emerson's famous metaphor in "Nature" of ecstatic perception as a "transparent eyeball" incorporating "the currents of the Universal Being" and reflecting "the lover of uncontained and immortal beauty." At the same time, he also remains aware of what Emerson in a later essay ("Experience") called the "evanescence and lubricity of all objects" that renders such instants of ideal perception so tragically transient. To choose still other analogies to approach by way of indirection Malick's unique contribution to the war movie, his film treads the thin red line between cinematic realism and expressionism, between Welsh's "rock" and Witt's "beautiful light."

Their second dialogue, set in the lush green grass at "the magic hour" at the precise midpoint of the film, begins with a beautiful, balanced two-shot and Welsh's promising note of compassion ("I feel sorry for you, kid"), but this putatively intimate "conversation" turns out to be a monologue, punctuated by four identical shots of the silent Witt, calmly absorbing Top's skepticism and the approaching tropical darkness. "You're just running into a burning house," Welsh's catechism begins, "and nobody can be saved. What difference you think you can make, one single man in all this madness? If you die, it's gonna be for nothing." As his sergeant concludes by again denying the existence of some other ideal world, insisting on "just this rock," for the fourth time Witt stares ahead with a soft smile, then raises his gaze as Malick cuts to a gorgeous long shot of a tall palm absorbing the first light of the rising moon. But the scene ends (or perhaps the next scene begins) with another formally composed landscape in the silvery light, a companion image of wild dogs feasting on the carrion of war. This sight, equally beautiful in its own way, reflects Welsh's world, confirmed by voiceover later in the film: "War doesn't ennoble men. It turns them into dogs."

Their final exchange occurs in a burned-out house, recalling Welsh's metaphor and the striking shot at the beginning of the film where Witt describes his mother's deathbed and the camera cranes up the bedroom wall to reveal an open blue sky. Malick confirms the connection between these two scenes by repeating the camera movement upward to show the sky through the ruined roof and by fixing again on the image of a

birdcage, earlier seen housing a parakeet in the mother's room but now, with cage door opened, vacant. After some initial verbal parrying, Witt confronts his sergeant's mocking attitude, using the same metaphor Top had invoked in their last meeting: "You care about me, don't you, sergeant? I always felt like you did. Why do you always make yourself out like a rock?" Welsh does not reply, as Witt had not answered why he was such a troublemaker at the beginning of the scene, but soon the men do respond to each other's questions. "Do you ever feel lonely?" Witt asks, to which Welsh sardonically answers, "Only when I'm with people." As the dialogue concludes, Welsh calls Witt a "magician" for preserving his idealism and asks him, "You still believing in the beautiful light, are you?" Witt remains steadfast in his faith: "I still see a spark in you." It remains a strangely moving scene (far different from the detachment and irony that marked Malick's films of the 1970s and were often used to describe *The Thin Red Line*), both a self-revealing colloquy—the director reflecting on his own magical manipulation of light—and a religious dialogue between an existentialist and a saint. The offscreen monologue that concludes *The Thin Red Line* over the collective portrait and close-ups of C Company's survivors, the last of seemingly "endless modulations of a single face" (Schaffer), articulates for a final time the synthesis that Malick's film has continually sought to present. It begins with elemental questions reminiscent of Whitman's great poem, "Song of Myself" ("A child said *What is the grass?*" [sec. 6]) and ends virtually quoting Wordsworth's "The Prelude" ("Tumult and peace, the darkness and the light— / Were all like workings of one mind, the features / Of the same face" [VI; 636–38]): "Where is it that we were together? Who were you that I lived with, walked with? Darkness and light, strife and love, are they the workings of one mind, the features of the same face? O my soul, let me be with you now. Look out through my eyes, look out at the things you made. All things shining."

For one of the few times in the film, Malick provides language commensurate with his images, a kind of benediction suggesting a peace that passes understanding. The soldiers his camera scans during most of the monologue, with the exception of Sergeant Welsh, are deliberately anonymous. The speaking voice is similarly difficult to recognize, especially since it belongs to none of the men observed on the ship. It proves to be (after several viewings) Witt, still asking questions from beyond the grave, like Dante at the end of *The Divine Comedy* or Chaucer's Troilus in *Troilus and Criseyde*. Now an occupant of the "other world" gazing down on Welsh, who is still in his "moving box" in "this world," among his comrades, Witt's spirit can bask in the "beautiful light" that renders all of creation one unified, brilliant whole.

Although *The Thin Red Line* is not nearly as self-reflexive as Malick's first two films, it does seem significant that the narrative concludes with this reference to *looking*, followed immediately by a reprise of the native rhythmic chorus heard at the beginning. The last phrase, "all things shining," conjures the luminescence of the silver screen and may suggest that the spiritual realm Witt has been ever drawn to might correspond to the creative impulse of the artistic imagination (Silberman 169). Malick's poetic cinema has always aspired to this realm, even while depicting the tawdry lives of two semiliterate outlaws in *Badlands* or the exhausting labor of migrant workers in *Days of Heaven*. As in his previous films, the otherworldly music that accompanies the exotic images sounds the possibility of another dimension of human experience, an escape from the quotidian.

"The Unanswered Question"

Malick's two recent films test the patience and intelligence of contemporary audiences by sacrificing some elements of narrative structure to pursue certain comprehensive philosophical problems. In *The Thin Red Line*, this inquiry synthesizes Christian faith with Buddhist ideas; in *The New World* (after Malick had become increasingly interested in the Melanesian community late in the production of his war film), the religious element derives from Native American cultures. Ron Mottram has noted how, "more than the first two films, *The Thin Red Line* transcends the immediate setting and action of the narrative to ask questions that penetrate to the heart of the Western mythos, such as the source and nature of evil, the existence of the spiritual, and the role and meaning of love" (19). Following the film's most brutal scene of hand-to-hand combat, Zimmer's orchestral score modulates into Charles Ives's haunting 1906 composition for trumpet, flute, and string quartet, "The Unanswered Question," as Witt roams the burning village giving comfort to the emaciated Japanese prisoners and Private Dale sadistically torments a captured soldier. "I'm going to sink my teeth into your liver," Dale sneers. "You're dying. See them birds up there? You know they eat you raw. Where you're going, you're not coming back from." The Japanese responds, at first plaintively, in his own language, then, after Dale sticks some cigarette butts up his nose to offset the stench, in more threatening tones. Neither man can understand the other; there are no subtitles (as there were in a prior scene inside the Japanese machine-gun nest), but the essence of the exchange can hardly be lost. Poisoned by war, Dale's immediate response is to deny any relation to his prisoner. In voiceover, he repudiates the dying soldier's humanity: "What are you to me? Nothing." A few scenes later, however, the prisoner's incomprehensible words—"Kisamawa shinundayo" (You too will die) (Chion 60)—return to Dale, now isolated from his comrades, shivering uncontrollably (as had the conquered Japanese) and crying in the tropical rain.

Ives's theme, like the untranslated Japanese heard again in the crucial moment when Witt is surrounded by the camouflaged enemy, speaks in a somewhat strange musical idiom that nonetheless manages to communicate what the composer called "the perennial question of existence" (Swafford 180). In both instances in the film, the Japanese phrases refer to life and death: "I don't want to kill you. Surrender," the lead soldier tells Witt at gunpoint (Chion 61). Malick's entire project can be understood as the effort to pose eternal, unanswerable questions through a new, essentially nonverbal, and often mysterious cinematic language. Viewed in this way, the lengthy metaphysical questions repeatedly spoken by different but often indistinguishable voices on the sound track become more significant for their mellifluousness than for their intellectual content.

Witt alone seems to apprehend the common humanity that connects him to the "enemy," first in his acts of compassion after the violent raid and finally in the calm with which he contemplates his end. The Japanese platoon, festooned with tree branches, nearly blends in with the verdant landscape as they approach him. The camera tracks back, as if in awe of Witt's silent passivity in the face of death. His expression might mean many things, but it is devoid of agony or complaint. Emerson's poem "The Sphinx," which speaks of "meaning sublime" that reconciles pleasure and pain, provided the title for Ives's "The Unanswered Question"; *The Thin Red Line* also seems inspired by Emerson's poetry as well as his more famous essays. "Brahma" begins with a stanza that applies to the aftermath of the Americans' victorious assault and to Witt's sacrificial end:

If the red slayer think he slays,
    Or if the slain think he is slain,
They know not well the subtle ways
    I keep, and pass, and turn again.

Malick creates a startling correlative to Emerson's poem when, for the only time, he employs voiceover to express the feelings—in English—of the Japanese, a dead soldier, buried except for his impassive face gazing at the GI looking down at him: "Are you righteous, kind? Does your confidence lie in this? Are you loved by all? Know that I was, too." Or perhaps it is Whitman again whom the filmmaker is recalling in this scene, another poem from *Drum-Taps:*

—I dwell not on soldier's perils or soldier's joys.
But in silence, in dreams' projections,
While the world of gain and appearance and mirth goes on.
　　("The Wound-Dresser")

So much of *The Thin Red Line* conveys Whitman's sense of the dreamlike quality of war (through muffled sound, slow motion, strange landscapes, and the juxtaposition of incongruous images and polyphonic voices) along with Emerson's sense of eternal transformation and transcendent nature.

Malick's film, like poetry (and unlike philosophy), responds to the unanswerable questions of all men under stress in the universal language of music and images. More precisely, its "questions *about* the world are coupled with different ways of *looking at* the world" (Bersani and Dutoit 143). As the camera follows Welsh looking after his men in the lush green twilight, a voiceover—not Welsh's but Witt's—comments on the subjectivity of all human vision: "One man looks at a dying bird and thinks there's nothing but unanswered pain. Another man sees that same bird and feels the glory." *The Thin Red Line* is filled with images of birds—a close-up of a wounded sparrow early on, the vultures that Dale points out to the dying Japanese soldier, the soaring flocks that Welsh observes at Witt's gravesite, the pair of tropical parrots at the beginning and at the very end—all suggesting different possibilities of meaning. After the terrifying battle, after Bell receives his wife's terrible Dear John letter ("Oh my friend of all those *shining* years!" [italics mine]), Malick concludes the sequence with two lyrical images, visual codas for these

two events: a carefully composed long shot of Bell walking away among the oil drums as a jet fighter gracefully lands on the newly captured airstrip, followed by a shimmering still life of a gently billowing lace curtain that decorated his bedroom at home. These distilled moments of intensified perception gather their own meanings, each according to the viewer's disposition.

The film begins with an equally evocative image: a crocodile entering the green slime of a tropical river. Most critics have interpreted this initial shot as representing the director's "obsessive central myth of Eden before and after the Fall" (Martin). The accompanying ominous minor chord, followed by the creature's descent into the ooze and the first question spoken in voiceover ("What's this war in the heart of nature?"), suggest that the ensuing narrative will be about Paradise lost. The images that immediately follow, however, call this assumption into question. Are we to see the brilliant shafts of light beaming through the treetops and the wondrous designs of the foliage as signs of a benevolent, inviolate nature? Or are we to observe instead the tangled vines that threaten to strangle the trees, the same phenomenon that Tall points out to Staros much later in the film to illustrate nature's cruelty? Long before the Ives theme is introduced, Malick has begun his film with an unanswered question. Even the status of the crocodile as a significant symbol is deliberately called into question when, away from the line, the victorious GIs celebrate the capture of a far less threatening crocodile displayed on the back of an army truck.

The inquiring voice opening the film turns out to belong to Witt, blissfully AWOL in his Pacific paradise. Malick cuts abruptly from scenes of Witt paddling a canoe in the still waters and enjoying the company of the natives to a shot of the approaching patrol boat that will take him back to the warship and the interview with Welsh in the brig. Witt's sudden removal from this Peaceable Kingdom to imposed duty as a stretcher bearer (a reprieve from court-martial Welsh has arranged on his behalf) re-creates a circumstance similar to the impressment of Billy Budd in Melville's last novel. Like Billy, the "handsome sailor," Witt seems to embody the ideal in his physical beauty as well as his moral innocence, a beatific presence in the midst of a violent and anxious world. Much of the suspense of Melville's and Malick's narratives hangs on the question of what will happen to such apparent human goodness in the midst of "this great evil." Both Billy and Witt are sacrificed in the end, enduring their deaths with extraordinary composure. The fallen world of war and its attendant duty cannot sustain their mortal lives, although their spirits seem to ascend in a kind of apotheosis. Thus, *The Thin Red Line* concludes with Welsh's surprising prayer that he might "feel the lack" and Witt's benediction on "all things shining."

Each of Malick's four films to date, in retrospect, expresses a kind of separation anxiety, not only from Paradise but from persons with whom one seemed to share a destiny. In *The Thin Red Line* this motif can be found in Bell's desperate clinging to memories of his wife; in Staros's departure from his men, whom he describes (first in Greek) as his "sons"; in Welsh's response to Witt's death; and most clearly in Witt's removal from the communal experiences on the Edenic island. Perhaps this theme, which becomes much more prominent in the two most recent films, comes naturally to a man who has been separated from family, country, and career for two decades and who apparently remains, like Sergeant Welsh, lonely only when he is around people. In any case, the ideas of dispersal and dissolution are never far from the center of his next film, *The New World*.

The New World

"The Last Mohican"

With the completion of *The New World*, Malick not only fulfilled his ambition of filming the Pocahontas–John Smith story, a script he had written in the 1970s, but reaffirmed his reputation as "the film poet of [the New Hollywood] generation" (Mast and Kawin 356). The visual beauty of the widescreen images, much of which was captured by the rare use of 65mm film, the drastically reduced dialogue, much of which is barely comprehensible as a result of the actors wearing microphones as well as speaking in exotic British accents and frequently unsubtitled Algonquin language, and the lyrical quality of the multiple voiceovers, expressive because of their tone as much as their content, combine to produce a spectacle that bedazzled admirers and benumbed detractors. Although its status in the canon of world cinema or even the span of Malick's oeuvre has yet to be determined, two things about *The New World* seem certain:

1) along with continuities with various features of the films of the 1970s, it clearly stands as a counterpart to *The Thin Red Line* in comparison to the diptych of *Badlands* and *Days of Heaven*; 2) it defines once again Malick's commitment to an idiosyncratic style of moviemaking that has certified him as the reclusive "genius" of American cinema.

In an exemplary essay on Malick's achievement with the release of *The New World*, David Sterritt described the director as "a last Mohican for the personal-epic mode pioneered in the 1970s by the likes of Francis Ford Coppola (*Apocalypse Now*) and Michael Cimino (*The Deer Hunter*), who had the resourcefulness to obtain—and the audacity to risk—many millions of other people's dollars on highly intuitive, even eccentric visions" (12). The analogy is well chosen, as it evokes Malick's nearly anachronistic cinematic aspirations while alluding to James Fenimore Cooper's Leatherstocking novels, which share some of *The New World*'s themes as well as its elegiac, slightly dated style, and (perhaps unintentionally) to Michael Mann's action-adventure *The Last of the Mohicans* (1992), which serves (along with Disney's 1995 animated blockbuster *Pocahontas*) as a kind of foil to Malick's reconstruction of America's colonial history. The two earlier movies, if they did not simply render *The New World* redundant, certainly hampered its chances for commercial success, as did the casting of an Irish actor, Colin Farrell, and a fourteen-year-old amateur, Q'orianka Kilcher, in the lead roles.

Compared to *The Last of the Mohicans* or *Pocahontas*—or to the Oscar-winning *Dances with Wolves*, for that matter—*The New World* is an art film through and through, subordinating dramatic structure and dialogue to stunning visual compositions, imposing restrictions on lighting, cinematography, and computer-generated effects, and complicating moral or ideological judgments about the characters. These qualities more clearly link Malick's film to Bruce Bereford's earlier depiction of the Encounter—in this case, the French Jesuits' attempt to convert the Hurons of Quebec—in *Black Robe* (1991). In addition to their concern with personal transcendence, both epics employ historical maps in the opening credits and subordinate dramatic development and the construction of character to sublime images of the natural world and dialogue that centers on spiritual truths. Not surprisingly, neither film triumphed at the box office.

Once again, the director himself took no part in the marketing of his $40 million film. He is nowhere to be found on the official website or the DVD, both of which include extensive features on the making of *The New World* but no images of Malick. Such inaccessibility, of course, has become integral to the Malick persona, another index of his presumed genius, which putatively requires isolation from the crass corporate executives who control the American movie industry and the philistines who constitute the American movie audience. It seems unlikely, however, given his own remarks on the characters of *Badlands* (see the interviews in this volume), the repeated testimony of colleagues and friends, or his choice of popular story lines and practice of budgetary responsibility, that Terrence Malick the person actually conforms to the stereotype of the isolated, misunderstood American "Artist of the Beautiful"—the title of one of Hawthorne's best stories—although the legend about him persists. Thus, the scholar Ron Mottram begins his essay by describing the director, not inaccurately, as one "who has avoided being swallowed up in the desperate enterprise of American commercial cinema and who has truly moved to the sound of a different drummer" (13). Such appraisals, compounded by reviewers of *The New World* and infatuated acolytes on the Internet, while they certainly speak to Malick's artistic sensibility and integrity, have the unfortunate effect of dominating critical analysis of the films themselves.

To a degree largely ignored by reviewers, *The New World* is Malick's most personal film, but it also remains remarkably consistent with the themes and imagery of his earlier work, particularly *The Thin Red Line.* Both recent films feature large casts and exotic settings. The director resumes his experiments with voiceover, reducing the multiple, sometimes indistinguishable speakers of the previous film to three clearly distinct persons (Pocahontas, Smith, and John Rolfe) but continuing to have these voices meditate and speculate rather than to narrate or explain. The carefully composed long takes again emphasize the classical elements of earth, air, fire, and water, sometimes employing particular images (low-angle shots of sunlight piercing the treetops, native villages in flames, clear streams flowing over smooth stones) that seem almost interchangeable with *The Thin Red Line.* As is true of all three prior films, these natural images are accompanied by an expressive original score, punctuated by significant passages of classical music (Satie in *Badlands*, Saint-Saëns in

Days of Heaven, Ives in *The Thin Red Line,* Wagner and Mozart here). The characters, although obviously individuated by virtue of their historical significance, remain, by virtue of the values they embody as well as their unspoken names (except for Smith's), representative and lacking psychological depth. It may be only a slight exaggeration to describe *The New World* as a "prequel" to Malick's war film.

The opening scene of Newport's ships arriving at Jamestown parallels the invasion of Guadalcanal in *The Thin Red Line.* Like the World War II soldiers, the English settlers embark on a struggle for survival in a verdant but dangerous environment populated by strange, potentially hostile natives of a different race. Captain Smith, in particular, bears comparison with Private Witt, both "rebellious military men drawn to the ways of indigenous peoples and their communion with nature" (Major) yet doomed by their own sense of service to the state. Compared with the films of the 1970s, *The Thin Red Line* and *The New World* together reflect a shift in their creator's thematic concerns from philosophical inquiry to religious faith; thus, both films conclude on a note of prayer and worshipful reconciliation. Sergeant Welsh, recovered from the bitterness expressed at Witt's graveside, sounds chastened in his final voiceover, assuming for the only time a tone of supplication: "If I never meet you in this life, let me feel the lack." Pocahontas, content in the face of her own death knowing that her child shall survive, reaches peace in her own reverent last words: "Mother, now I know where you live." By seeming to affirm a soulful connection to humanity and a spiritual bond with (Mother) Nature, Malick takes his romantic stand with the Last Mohicans of the art film, a cinema of beauty and ideas, against the incursions of a younger generation of cinematic cavalrymen represented by Quentin Tarantino and Christopher Nolan.

Malick had been working with Benicio del Toro for some time on a biopic about Che Guevara when the project foundered for lack of financing. On the recommendation of Michael Barker, the co-president of Sony Pictures Classics, he called the independent producer Sarah Green, and the two struck up a partnership that led to the filming of his twenty-five-year-old script for what would become, four years later, *The New World.* The production itself was time-consuming (seventeen weeks) and arduous. The production designer Jack Fisk, who had served Malick in that capacity for each of the three previous films, built a replica of the original fort at Jamestown using only wood from the local forests. The actors were required to lose weight and, in the case of the "naturals" (as the American Indians are called in the film), to learn the defunct Algonquin language. The Mexican cinematographer Emmanuel Lubezki, like Almendros and Toll before him, was instructed to shoot using only available light with handheld cameras or Steadicams almost exclusively. The costumes, props, and makeup (principally tattooing and body painting for the Indians) were prepared with meticulous attention to detail and historical accuracy. Only a single shot in the entire film was computer generated to reproduce the appearance of an extinct Carolina parakeet. (Malick is reputed to be an avid birder.) Farrell was twenty-eight at the time of filming, the same age as Smith when he arrived at Jamestown; Kilcher was fourteen, only a year or two older than Pocahontas when the English landed.

For all the attention to historical accuracy and narrative verisimilitude, however, the film's central love story—the magnetic attraction between Smith the military adventurer and Pocahontas the native princess—is almost certainly a product of myth modified by Malick's imagination. "'First and foremost,'" Sarah Green repeatedly emphasized in marketing the film, "'we've created a love story'" (qtd. in Sterritt B12). Historians generally discount the likelihood of a romance, principally because of the Indian girl's youth, and so the director's poetic license with the facts might seem a concession to popular taste, even an instance of the supposedly uncompromising artist selling out in pursuit of commercial success. Nevertheless, the love story does provide the film with a necessary dramatic structure and allows Malick to continue his meditation on the subject of love—love, not sex (although each of his four films contains love scenes, they remain remarkably chaste, for different reasons)—that so engaged him in the character of Private Bell in *The Thin Red Line,* just as his new interest in indigenous cultures in that film also gets fully developed in *The New World.*

The film's opening credits suggest by metonymy the narrative's blending of factual detail with subjective interpretation, confirming Vlada Petric's observation in his review of *Days of Heaven* about Malick's poetic vision of history and geography (40). While the locations, spatial relationships, and physical landscapes of his first two films were often deliberately imprecise or uncertain (for example, the proximity of the billboard in

Badlands to the town and the highway or the distance between Bill and the buffalo herd in *Days of Heaven*), the assault on Hill 210 involves careful reference to coordinate points on a military field map, and *The New World* begins with sweeping close-ups of seventeenth-century maps of Virginia. As the camera pans in a style reminiscent of the credit sequence in *Days of Heaven* (not to mention *Black Robe*), the inky lines of the rivers swell with blue water, like veins coursing with blood, animating the map of the New World, bringing it to life in response to Pocahontas's invocation: "Come Spirit. Help us in this story of our land."

As was the case in his previous pictures, Malick's representation of American history in *The New World* is filtered through the consciousness of his own history as well as contemporary events. The visual experience of the Vietnam War returns in the images of conquering white soldiers burning native villages. Separated by three and a half centuries, the scenes of fiery destruction at Guadalcanal and Virginia appear eerily similar within the two films. Because *The Thin Red Line* depicts the U.S. army's invasion of an Asiatic island, the associations with Vietnam come readily to mind when the GIs overrun the Japanese encampment; in *The New World,* however, a current conflict—the war in Iraq—provides the more immediate context for Malick's depiction of the clash of cultures. The origins of American hegemony and the shadow of 9/11 (perhaps reflected in the skeletal remains of the Indian longhouse) thus color and confound his film's development of the love story.

Judged strictly by the stark standards of box-office receipts and published reviews, *The New World* has proven to be the director's least successful film. Domestic grosses were less than $13 million; international

receipts brought the total to just over $30 million, approximately the production budget (exclusive of distribution and marketing). After delays for last-minute editing and following a very limited release at Christmas 2005, in time to qualify for the annual awards, Malick withdrew the film to make additional cuts of about seventeen minutes (reducing the running time to 2:15) prior to a more general January release. A director's cut DVD in high definition, restoring the cuts and including additional footage, is currently being prepared by Warner, leaving viewers with three different versions of *The New World*. Needless to say, the director himself will not offer commentary or appear in the features of the expanded disc. While the new version may kindle a reassessment of Malick's achievement (or creative intentions) and bring the film's revenues closer to the break-even point, it seems more likely to become a collector's item than the definitive text that its producers envision.

Critical response to *The New World* was also generally disheartening. More discouraging than the predictable complaints about slow pace, pretentious imagery, incoherent voiceovers, empty dialogue, and wooden performances was the mocking tone that informed several reviews. With *The Thin Red Line,* nearly all the criticism was couched in respectful praise for the director's ambition and appreciation for his return. Now the negative phrases turned scornful: "just so much atmospheric tootle" (Stephanie Zacharek in *Salon*); "monumentally slight" (J. Hoberman in *The Village Voice*); "the slowest-pace film of the year" (Harvey S. Karten in *Arizona Reporter*); "'psychedelic and kooky'" (Roger Friedman [Foxnews .com] qtd. in Carter). In an echo of the reaction to Linda Manz in *Days of Heaven,* Kilcher alone was largely excluded from the condemnation, even when it came in the form of faint praise, as in Peter Rainer's restrained, thoughtful review in the *Christian Science Monitor* entitled "'World' Turns Slowly (but It Sure Is Pretty)." Reportedly chosen from among three thousand aspirants for the role, she is generally praised for her embodiment of sprightliness and uncanny maturity, providing the film with much of its narrative energy. Undoubtedly, the approval of her singular performance, as in the case of Manz, was influenced by her youth and nonprofessional status. Malick's part in shaping that performance, however, was largely ignored.

Many significant directors who have developed a unique personal style and examined recurrent themes, such as Ingmar Bergman, Yasujiro

Ozu, Eric Rohmer, and Woody Allen, have been subjected to similar mocking appraisals at some stage of their careers. While the parodic references to Malick's obsessive images and cinematic practices do little to illuminate a particular film's inherent qualities, they do impinge (along with the box-office figures) on his future viability as a filmmaker. *The New World* has not yet received the detailed scrutiny its epic scope, visual and aural design, and thematic complexity require, nor has its visceral impact been adequately acknowledged. While Malick himself remains aloof from criticism of his work, Rainer seems right in suggesting at the end of his mixed review that "[w]e may need him more than he needs us."

When Malick is dismissed by critics it is generally for two reasons: 1) he sacrifices cinematic movement for static compositions of self-conscious gorgeousness, thereby confusing the movie theater with an art gallery; 2) because of this absorption in abstract beauty and ideas, he cannot tell a story. The first criticism seems patently absurd, given the cinema's visual basis, something like Salieri's complaint (in *Amadeus*) about Mozart's music: "Too many notes." The second contains some truth in regard to Malick's deliberate pacing, subordination of psychological insights as a narrative hook, and deviations from conventional dramatic structure. But in his most recent film, he has not one but several stories to tell, each of them richly and coherently developed.

The Epic

The most obvious of these stories is the eponymous one of the foundation of the nation, the establishment of the first permanent English colony in the New World at Jamestown in 1607. Because Malick can rely on the viewer's knowledge of the essential historical facts, particularly the tale of the American Indian princess imploring her father Powhatan to spare the English captive's life, he eschews the usual exposition, omitting, for example, the names of the expedition's leader, Christopher Newport (Christopher Plummer), or individuals among the tribe of naturals that gathers in wonder at the sight of three large ships entering Trinity Harbor. Malick films the opening sequence in a style similar to Herzog's portrayal of Pizarro's descent from the clouds in *Aguirre, Wrath of God,* employing natural sounds and solemn music to accompany the westerners' perilous adventure into unknown territory.

Heralded by the sounds of diegetic chirps of crickets and tropical birds and Wagner's overture to *Das Rheingold* incorporated into James Horner's score, the English fleet anchors and the colonists enter the frame through a lush green meadow, exactly like the GIs landing at Guadalcanal, weapons drawn. "This place will serve," Newport declares (in words that may suggest Brigham Young's pronouncement upon arriving in Utah more than two centuries later), and sets forth the group's mission in phrases that anticipate the myth of the American Adam and the spirit of capitalism: "We shall make a new start, a fresh beginning. Here the blessings of earth are bestowed upon all. We shall build a true commonwealth, hard work and self-reliance our virtue." This speech, with its democratic principles and proscription against conquest or commercial profit ("We are not here to pillage and raid"), echoes the idealism of the later New England colonists—indeed, the fleet led by the *Susan Constant* might serve equally as the Pilgrims' *Mayflower* so far as the film is concerned—but these lofty aims immediately give way to the challenges of physical survival and, following a nearly disastrous winter, the distractions of commerce.

In his first voiceover, Smith describes the naturals as "like a herd of curious deer" and, after being spared by their chief, as "gentle, loving, faithful, lacking all guile and trickery." These qualities, which coincide with Jean-Jacques Rousseau's romantic eighteenth-century formulation of the noble savage, prove dangerous to both parties when a native, unaware of English property rights, walks off with a colonist's hatchet and is promptly shot, setting off an initial round of hostilities. Smith returns to the fort after his sojourn among the Powhatan tribe with a diplomatic message: "Though the naturals lived in peace, yet they were strong and would not suffer their land to be taken away." A vicious battle ensues once Powhatan recognizes that the English do not intend to leave, and in terrible fighting (reminiscent of scenes from *The Thin Red Line*) Pocahontas's brother is killed, his dying vision repeating another Malick low-angle shot of sunlight piercing the treetops. The ultimate outcome of the cultural struggle, of course, is inevitable—colonization of the New World requires conquest—but unlike the classical Western or its contemporary form (see *Dances with Wolves*), the film remains close to ideologically neutral. Neither Newport nor Smith is a traitorous Aguirre, a Hitler figure bent on outrageous conquest and personal glory;

the villains among the English are easily repulsed by their own leaders. Malick aligns himself with the naturals, to be sure, and empathizes in particular with Pocahontas's predicament, trapped between familial loyalty and nascent love ("You have walked blindly into a situation you did not anticipate," her husband John Rolfe tells her near the end of the film), but he does not condemn the colonists (soldiers on both sides are equally violent; both societies cultivate domestic tranquility) and seems to identify with Smith's conflicted feelings.

In addition to the struggle for possession of the land, the epic story involves the clash between contrasting attitudes towards nature, the natives' pantheistic coexistence within a landscape imbued with divine spirit versus the colonists' anticipation of a "post-Enlightenment ideal of taming and harnessing nature to accomplish humanly determined goals" (Sterritt 12). In depicting this cultural divide, symbolized early in the film by the compass Smith shows the Indians and later embodied in the figure of the transformed princess learning English letters and wearing European shoes, *The New World* resembles previous films about attempts to civilize "savage" subjects such as François Truffaut's *The Wild Child* (1969) and Werner Herzog's *The Mystery of Kasper Hauser* (1975). Pocahontas proves more compliant with the ways of her adopted society than these later historical figures—"Am I as you like?" she asks of Smith in a touching reunion at the English fort—but Malick brilliantly envisions the uncertainty of her cultural assimilation in two matched shots, one at the middle and the other at the end, of the native princess, garbed in English dress, standing in a tall tree. In these images as well as those of her cavorting in the formal gardens at court at

the end of the film, Malick reflects the native woman's total assimilation within *nature* rather than the social world.

The story of Pocahontas's marriage to the tobacco farmer John Rolfe (Christian Bale), her invitation to the court of King James, and her untimely death at Gravesend is often dropped from her role in the Jamestown epic, almost certainly because it disrupts the sentimental, optimistic theme of her rescue of Smith and the consequent development of the American nation. Malick includes it in his film—in fact, he makes it central to the narrative's overall effect—in keeping with historical truth but also to complicate his epic. The London episode reveals that for the ever-receptive Pocahontas/Rebecca, the Old World becomes the New World. Her curious gaze at the black man in the marketplace or the caged raccoon at court mirrors the English royalty's appraisal of "the New World's Princess," as she is announced to the king, herself the object of international curiosity. Her serenity in the midst of such exotic vistas— even her placid interview with the weary Smith—redeems a pledge she made to herself when first exiled from her own people: "I will find joy in all I see." It is a pledge that Malick's cinema has persistently confirmed by seeking not to master nature by examining and recording it but rather, in Emerson's phrase, by wearing the colors of its spirit ("Nature") as the Native Americans once did.

The Creation Myth

Malick has rarely been described as a religious filmmaker, but *The New World* begins where *The Thin Red Line* left off, with an invocation to the glory of creation. Soon after the English arrive, a band of tribesmen encounters a cross that the colonists have erected, just as the GIs pass by a statue of Buddha on the trail leading up Hill 210. All cultures, these moments suggest, share the impulse to worship some greater power that guides human lives. Christian iconography and sacramental images recur throughout Malick's oeuvre: Kit's Christlike pose with rifle slung across his shoulders; the blessings at the beginning and end of harvest; Abby's Orthodox wedding to the Farmer; Pocahontas's baptism as Rebecca. In *The New World* he takes up again the biblical story of Eden and the Fall, positing as in his previous film (and also in the fresh starts for Linda and Abby at the end of *Days of Heaven*) the possibility of redemption (even Kit asks at the end of *Badlands*, "Think they'll take

that into consideration?" wondering whether he can avoid "the juice").
Malick's current project, *Tree of Life*, might, judging by the title and current conjectures, bring him back to Genesis and what might be called his obsessive theme of man's exile from a Paradise that yet surrounds him. Although *The New World* is clearly an epic, the recounting of the creation of a new civilization, it can also be called a retelling of this central myth in Christian thought, Genesis, the story of Paradise lost and perhaps still to be regained.

"We rise from out of the soul of thee," Pocahontas prays to Mother Earth before the title credits begin, raising her arms skyward as if to bring the film itself into being. The story then commences with a series of underwater shots, first of fish gliding in front of the camera (as in *Days of Heaven*), followed by a small group of swimmers led by Pocahontas shimmering in the blue water (as in the opening of *The Thin Red Line*). The last of the underwater shots portrays several tribesmen kneeling on the shoreline and pointing to the distance as the princess ascends to the surface, followed by a dissolve to a crane shot above the waters as the English fleet enters the scene. Through cinematic metonymy, this prologue depicts a kind of phylogenesis of the evolution of mankind, a process that the narrative will recapitulate through the life of Pocahontas. Malick's adaptation of the Darwinian creation story, however, hardly follows the popularized notion of the Ascent of Man; rather, the film explores the elusive ideal of a harmonious synthesis of wilderness and cultivation, pantheism and Christianity, native culture and Western civilization.

Like Witt in the brig, John Smith is first seen imprisoned in the hold of the *Susan Constant*, gazing out from the darkness through the porthole at the activities beyond (a favorite Malick framing device, first seen in the views from inside the bunkhouse in *Days of Heaven* and repeated at the end of *The New World* in the long shot through the gazebo). Newport frees him from the noose around his neck soon after the colonists land, charging him to "repair his reputation" by leading a scouting party upriver to meet the native king. Smith's path to personal redemption begins with his immersion in the forest stream, a natural baptism that corresponds visually to the low-angle shots of Pocahontas in the treetops, rendering them both almost undistinguishable from the natural environment. Captured by the Indians and taken as prisoner (again) to their chief, Smith discovers in his lengthy sojourn after Pocahontas's life-saving intercession—the climax of the folk legend occurs barely twenty-five minutes into the film—a utopian existence among the naturals that represents for Malick not the historical reality but a spiritual ideal. "They have no jealousy, no sense of possession." In short, Smith has discovered Eden in the New World. And in the preternatural princess, he has also found his spiritual mate, his unfallen Eve.

Smith's second reprieve from death, though it brings about his own "days of heaven," carries additional responsibilities. He must return to the fort, blindfolded so as not to retrace the direction, charged by Powhatan to ensure that the white settlers will leave in spring. Exiled from Paradise, he becomes a prisoner for a third time, having been tried in absentia by the diseased, dissolute survivors of the colony. "It was a dream," Smith recalls in voiceover his interlude with the tribe. "Now I am awake." Saved from certain starvation after Pocahontas leads a party of naturals bringing food, the Jamestown community barely lasts the winter, their numbers reduced from 103 to about thirty. Betrayed by the English and bereft after seeing the princess again, Smith wavers between two worlds and imagines being born again: "That fort is not the world. Start over. Exchange this false life for a new one. Give up the name of Smith." Why does he not desert the colony and start a new life among the naturals? Although his reasoning and motives are never made explicit ("What holds you here?" he asks himself), his ultimate decision marked only by the anguished gesture of overturning a table, he remains with the company out of the same sense of duty as Private

Witt, the nomadic soldier of *The Thin Red Line,* a deep-rooted desire, as Witt puts it, to be there "in case something bad happens."

It is the destiny of a fallen world for something bad to happen, and so a fierce battle ensues in which Pocahontas's brother is killed. The princess is subsequently exiled by Powhatan for warning the fort of the impending Indian attack. "Forgive me, father," she begs the grieving chief, thereby acknowledging her sin and inaugurating her own journey towards redemption. With Smith put in chains once again, this time for refusing to take Pocahontas hostage to protect the beleaguered fort, then released by Newport to return to England at King James's request, the narrative turns its attention to the exiled Indian girl, sold to the colony for a copper kettle, and her entry into her own new world. By the midpoint of the film, Malick has presented several permutations of the Genesis story: the colonists' migration from England in search of a "kingdom of the spirit," as Newport describes it in specifically biblical terms ("God has given us a Promised Land"); Smith's happiness in and expulsion from a natural Eden; Pocahontas's rebirth after being exiled as well, then her struggle to transform her transgression and displacement into a Fortunate Fall.

"When I first saw her," the new voice of John Rolfe declares two-thirds through the film, "she was regarded as someone finished, broken." The princess, baptized as Rebecca, seems inconsolable in her grief over her brother's death, her separation from her father, but, most devastatingly, over the departure and reported death of Captain Smith. Rolfe, too, knows grief, having buried his wife and only child. Drawn to Rebecca, he invites her to work in his tobacco fields, where she slowly begins to heal. "A nature like yours," he tells her, "can turn sorrow into good." The remainder of *The New World* is largely devoted to depicting the flowering of that goodness, inspired by prayer not from the catechism of her adopted religion but from her American Indian soul. Despite qualms about her lingering feelings for Smith, who she believes is dead, she marries the patient, sensitive Rolfe, and a child is born, for whom she gives thanks to the Great Sun. "Mother," she prays, "Show me a way. Teach me a path. Give me a humble heart."

Malick's film validates the sanctity and efficacy of her faith, which can be called neither pagan nor Christian but a synthesis of both, a *natural* religion. She indeed "rises" as the narrative progresses, achieving the

status of "the New World's Princess" as she regains a spiritual contentment evident in her pleasure in the royal gardens so apparently foreign
to her native land. While Smith has been thrice saved physically, his
spirit has been ravaged by his separation from the Edenic forest and
domestic joy; Pocahontas, in giving birth, has been born again. Her final
words pronounce a benediction that provides her story closure in the
same language as her invocation: "Mother, now I know where you live."
Unlike the restless, tormented Smith, who persists as a kind of Ishmael
in Malick's vision of his chase after the elusive West Indies, Pocahontas
in this closing scene, idealized by Malick's camera in the autumnal foliage and eulogized in Rolfe's voiceover, ascends to a state of grace.

The Love Story

For many viewers of *The Thin Red Line*, the scenes of Witt at ease in
the Melanesian village and the flashbacks to Bell's romantic memories
of his wife remain unwanted distractions from the central combat story,
but both of these subplots illustrate Malick's continuing interest in what
might be called the philosophy of love, an inquiry that can be felt in each
of his films. From Holly's perspective, *Badlands* is a love story ("Little by
little, we fell in love"): her retelling of her fatal attraction to a handsome
guy "from the wrong side of the tracks, so-called," despite the opposi-
tion of her father, reflects a high school sophomore's understanding
of *Romeo and Juliet*. In phrases that reverberate throughout Malick's
subsequent work, she describes how "each lived for the precious hours
when he or she could be with each other, away from the cares of the
world," and how the doomed lovers sensed that "we would never live
these days of happiness again, that they were lost forever." The tragedy,
in her eyes, is that their ideal of eternal love ("He wanted to die with
me, and I dreamed of being lost forever in his arms") cannot endure.
Love fades, as Woody Allen demonstrated in *Annie Hall* (1977), and so
Juliet eventually marries the son of her defense lawyer.

The love story in *The New World* also contains elements of *Romeo
and Juliet* ("He is not one of us," Powhatan warns his daughter about
the man from the wrong side of the ocean), but in its elaboration of a
philosophy of love, Malick's most recent film harkens back most clearly
to *Days of Heaven*. The triangular plot again involves a woman drawn to
men representing different kinds of love, the erotic attraction embodied

by the adventurer, Smith, versus the domesticated affections of the secure and stable Rolfe. As in *Days of Heaven,* Rolfe's courtship of Rebecca is initially hesitant; he comes to know her by observing her working his land and eventually inviting her to live with him. Like Abby, she agrees to marriage without wholly renouncing her first love. Even before she discovers the truth about Smith's fate, the divided self now called Rebecca prays to the god of her childhood, "Mother, why can I not feel as I should?" Upon learning that Smith is alive, she tells her husband, "I'm married to him," turning away from his caress. "You do not love me now," Rolfe tells her. "Someday you will." His love, it is clear by this assertion, amounts to faith, transcending the jealousy that torments and ultimately destroys the Farmer.

During their forest idyll together, Smith and the princess become worshippers of love, their voiceovers submitting totally to its claims.

SMITH: Love. Shall we deny it when it visits us? . . . There is only this. All else is unreal.
POCAHONTAS: A god he seems to me. What else is life but being near you. Do they suspect? I will be faithful to you, true. Two no more. One I am. I am.

A montage of close-ups (relatively rare in Malick's cinema) without any dialogue records the progress of their intense love, consecrated by the surrounding splendor of nature: cutaway shots of a lightning storm, the sky peeping through the treetops, a flock of migrating birds, ripples on a stream. These are their days of heaven.

Returned to the fort, plagued by its internal politics and the deadly hardships of winter, Smith's faith in the reality of his experiences among the Indians gives way to doubt. When Pocahontas leads a party bearing food to sustain the colonists, she asks him why he did not return to her. He replies at first with political advice, warning her not to put herself in danger with her own people. Then he tells her, "Don't trust me. You don't know who I am." Smith serves *The New World* something as Ishmael serves *Moby Dick,* an intermittent narrating consciousness doomed to a pseudonymous, nomadic existence that seems to derive from being a mystery to himself. The historical John Smith has proven to be a mystery to historians, his account of his adventures in Jamestown held suspect because of his habit of self-mythology. Malick's Smith knows he cannot be trusted because he knows he does not know himself. He vacillates in the middle of the film between submitting to the transformed Rebecca's steadfast devotion and the king's "plans" for his career. When, in his final conversation with Mrs. Rolfe, he finally realizes what he left behind in the forest, the recognition comes too late.

The girl's first love neither dies nor fades but is, in time, transformed, as the landscape around her changes with the seasons. "Love made the bond," her husband believes. "Love can break it, too." Her response to Rolfe's proposal of marriage carries the same honesty mixed with appreciation and hope as Abby's reply to the Farmer's declaration of love. "What a nice thing to say," Abby answers, without quite returning his emotion or saying yes to his offer. "I suppose we must be happy," Rebecca tells Rolfe, her solemn promise to become his wife. Five years later, after the birth of her son and her recognition of the sacrifice he is prepared to make to give her peace, she can say to her husband, "You are the man I thought you were, and more," words that surely remind her of John Smith's earlier warning about himself. Her farewell to Smith, like Abby's intimate conversation with Bill in the barn and Marty Bell's Dear John letter to her husband, gathers its poignancy not from the denial of love but from its acknowledgment and from the reverence for what they once shared.

The Personal Story

The ending of *The New World,* the closing scenes in London and at the royal court, conveys a different feeling from almost anything else in Malick's oeuvre. Far from the detachment generally ascribed to his filmmaking, this extended epilogue manages to create what might be called an emotional profundity by synthesizing the epic, religious, and romantic stories into narrative closure that stirs the senses and stimulates thought. Perhaps this effect results from the deliberate lyricism and retarded pace of the preceding hour—at great risk of losing many viewers' attention—but it also may be attributable to Malick's personal investment in the outcome. Given that the climax to the most popular aspect of the story, Pocahontas's intervention to save Smith's life, takes place so early, Malick clearly finds a deeper significance in the aftermath of this event, in the princess's cultural assimilation and role as ambassador to the capital of civilization and in Smith's lonely, frustrating career as a thwarted explorer of new worlds.

Malick's identification with Smith can be felt on several levels, beginning (admittedly a stretch) with the physical resemblance between the bearded, burly Colin Farrell and his director. Like Malick, Smith is portrayed as a natural leader and rebellious visionary, separated by talent and inclination from civilized society yet dependent on wealthy patrons to finance his ambition. (The historical Smith spent eleven years fruitlessly trying to raise sufficient funds to return to Virginia.) In the film's final episode, the prodigal adventurer returns to court on horseback, a Byronic hero still pursuing his dream but now uncertain whether it lies in the Indies or the Indian princess before him. His sparse dialogue with Mrs. Rolfe has a confessional tone similar to Bill's when he tells Abby, "I never knew what I had with you," but also perhaps expresses some particle of Malick's own regret at having been away for so long and having missed so much. "I thought it was a dream, what we knew in the forest," Smith says. "It's the only truth." Always generous—as she brought food to the starving colonists, she gives alms and a comforting touch to the paupers she encounters in London—the princess treats her first love with kindness and a sympathetic smile as she asks him, "Did you find your Indies, John?" There may be a note of irony in that question, but Malick also has her confirm the validity of his search when she adds, "You shall." In one of the most poignant exchanges in Malick's entire cinema, Smith quietly replies, "I may have sailed past them."

Even denying the autobiographical element in Smith's response, his self-reproach seems an unusual conclusion for such a romantic film (and filmmaker). Rarely in classic American literature does the hero find (or desire) fulfillment in marriage and the comforts of the hearth. Malick's philosophical musings in faraway places in his last two films would seem to align him with Melville's lofty assertion that "[i]n landlessness alone resides the highest truth" (*Moby Dick*, chapter 23), but *The New World* nevertheless closes with a paean to domestic bliss, as if Captain Ahab had returned to his young wife and child in Nantucket. When Rebecca rejoins her husband after bowing a silent goodbye to Smith, she embraces him in a close-up that foregrounds her wedding ring as she asks him if they may now go home. The camera next tracks lovingly around the hedges of the formal garden as she plays hide-and-seek with her son while the

Wagner overture swells on the sound track, replaced by Rolfe's voiceover as he writes about the death of his son's dear mother. After a filmography (including the first two hours of *The New World*) marked by alienation, migration, displacement, and the beckoning of the open road, Malick ends this odyssey with images of marital harmony (a still life of the marriage bed) and the stillness of nature. What this might suggest about the director's personal life and creative ambitions at a fairly advanced age must remain tentative without his own testimony, but within the film it seems a realistic concession to the processes of life, what Emerson and Thoreau had celebrated as the organic quality of nature.

In light of his sporadic directorial career, his current activities as a producer, and the ambitiousness of his work in progress, *Tree of Life*, it is tempting to speculate whether the closing sequence of *The New World* might not prove to be Malick's last cinematic testament. If so, it surely inscribes the major elements of his oeuvre to date. King James's court is but another permutation of the "big house," the seat of authority that his alienated protagonists must negotiate at their peril: Holly's yellow clapboard and the rich man's estate, the Farmer's Victorian mansion, General Quintard's warship, Powhatan's long house. Look closely: there is the birdcage again, housing a chicken in the London marketplace and the raccoon in the royal court. Rebecca and Smith stop in a gazebo by the side of a small stream, recalling Holly and Kit's picnic above the river, Abby and Bill's bathing and midnight tryst in the creek, and Marty's call to her husband to join her at the ocean's edge. The final image should not surprise: a low-angle shot of blue sky piercing the tall trees.

The most enduring of the concluding images in *The New World*, however, is the formal garden, which Malick manages to imbue with the qualities of Paradise both lost and regained. The anomalous appearance of the American Indian amidst the landscaped lawns, carefully trimmed trees and hedges, and classical statuary points to the Edenic days and nights in the forest that have been left behind not because of some Original Sin but because of the incursions of civilization. Opechancanough, Powhatan's designated emissary, gazes at the scene, touches the perfectly sculpted tree not with contempt but wonder. The long shots of the Old World garden with the Native American in the foreground record not only his displacement but also a beauty that remains, a *different* beauty.

The second of three scenes in these formal gardens depicts the parlay

between Smith and Rebecca. Although the views of the tree-lined walks and the gorgeous view from the gazebo across the river to the palace present spectacular man-made vistas, they represent for the enervated Smith a painful contrast to the paradise he once knew with Pocahontas in the Virginia woods. Only in the third of these scenes, Rebecca playing with her child and then cavorting alone, does Malick reconcile these uneasy moments with a vision of paradise regained. Fulfilling her promise to take joy in all she sees, the woman whose birth name means "playful one" (Petrakis 49) embodies something like the eternal human spirit as she merges with her environment, celebrates her family, and gives thanks for life. Although it is early autumn in the English gardens, and she is far from native soil and customs ("Who would have thought it?" Smith remarks of her new celebrity), she rejoices in her surroundings, at one with its colors, expressed in a spontaneous, unforgettable cartwheel.

Although the brevity of the Malick oeuvre allows for a reasonably comprehensive analysis of his four films to date, the temptation to total or evaluate his achievement remains problematic, not only because his work may not yet be finished but also because the films in question elude conventional generic descriptions and the director eschews all comment (at least since 1975) about his artistic intentions, preferring that his movies speak for themselves. This study, although scholarly and analytical, tends to dwell on what has been called "cinephiliac moments" (Keathley 30–36), images that amount to my own personal epiphanies while viewing Malick's films: the billboard scene in *Badlands*, the long shot of the train trestle in *Days of Heaven*, the dialogue at dusk in *The Thin Red Line*, the royal court sequence in *The New World*. These instances of cinematic plenitude seem to crystallize Malick's vision of a transcendent reality, replete with "the wonder of presence" (Jones, "Acts" 25) that defines the disorienting effect of his cinema.

Perhaps the director's sensibility is also registered in what his films have *not* displayed, in particular those elements that seem so pervasive in popular or postmodernist cinema. None of his films to date has disrupted the chronology of events in favor of nonlinear narrative; none has been marked by special effects or digital technologies; none has appealed to the taste for puzzles, or thrilling, nonstop action, or even simple suspense. These omissions suggest that, despite his reputation for opacity, Malick may be described as a remarkably *straightforward* filmmaker, content to create a revelatory "cinema in front of our eyes." This conviction about the presence of "another world" that can be projected on a large screen in a darkened auditorium may be why, at least for readers of this book, his next film (presumably *Tree of Life*, which is being shot in Texas at the time this is written) might still seem so fraught with significance.

Following the publication of *Moby Dick*, Herman Melville sent a remarkable letter to his friend Nathaniel Hawthorne in which he wrote, "Leviathan is not the biggest fish;—I have heard of Krakens" (567), referring to an even larger sea creature of Norse mythology. After the achievement of these four films, comprising a personal cinema of extraordinary beauty and seriousness, Malick has embarked on another prodigious project that has long occupied his imagination, shipped out on another artistic quest for krakens. Will this venture find its way to the screen; will there be another "Malick film"? We are lucky there have been four.

Interviews with Terrence Malick |

Reprinted here are the only two interviews with Terrence Malick that have been published to date, both in 1975 following the release of *Badlands*. They seem strikingly similar, as if the circumspect director had rehearsed the commentary he wished to be disseminated about his life and first film, yet Malick's remarks reveal several insights into his artistic intentions and literary sensibility as well as a bit of his personal philosophy. The interview with Beverly Walker appeared in *Sight and Sound* 44.2 (Spring 1975): 82–83; it is reprinted with permission of the British Film Institute. Michel Ciment's interview had been translated from English and published in the French journal *Positif* 170 (June 1975): 30–34. The original tape, unfortunately, is no longer available; the interview was translated back into English by Laura Reeck and published here with permission of the author.

Beverly Walker in *Sight and Sound*

Interviewing Terry Malick, producer-writer-director of *Badlands,* turned out, like his film, to be full of idiosyncratic surprises. My prepared list of questions went by the wayside as Malick talked with passion, conviction, and sometimes anger about his film. Acknowledging that he "couldn't have asked for more" in terms of critical acceptance, he also indicated that the actual filming was painful. Working in the dead heat of the 1972 summer, with a non-union crew and little money (three hundred thousand dollars, excluding some deferments to labs and actors), Malick encountered all sorts of problems, from difficulties over finance to the destruction of all the cameras during a fire sequence. Eventually, upon completion, Warners bought *Badlands* for just under a million dollars. It might turn in a decent profit for them.

The son of an oil company executive, Malick grew up in Texas and Oklahoma. He went to Harvard and later to Magdalen College, Oxford, as a Rhodes Scholar. Philosophy was his course of study, but he never completed his thesis—in fact, his topic wasn't even acceptable to his senior tutor, Gilbert Ryle. Summer jobs took him from the wheat harvests in America and Canada, to work in oilfields and driving a cement mixer in a railyard, to journalistic endeavors for *Life, Newsweek,* and the *New Yorker.* He was sent to Bolivia to observe the trial of Régis Debray; Che Guevara was killed the day after his arrival. In 1968, he was appointed a lecturer in philosophy for one year at MIT.

"I was not a good teacher; I didn't have the sort of edge one should have on the students, so I decided to do something else. I'd always liked movies in a kind of naïve way. They seemed no less improbable a career than anything else. I came to Los Angeles in the fall of 1969 to study at the AFI; I made a short called *Lanton Mills.* I found the AFI very helpful; it's a marvelous place. My wife was going to law school, and I was working for a time as a rewrite man—two days on *Drive, He Said,* five weeks on the predecessor to *Dirty Harry* at a time when Brando was going to do it with Irving Kershner directing. Then we all got fired by Warners; the project went to Clint Eastwood. I rewrote *Pocket Money* and *Deadhead Miles.* I got this work because of a phenomenal agent, Mike Medavoy.

"At the end of my second year there, I began work on *Badlands.* I wrote and, at the same time, developed a kind of sales kit with slides and videotape of actors, all with a view to presenting investors with something that would look ready to shoot. To my surprise, they didn't pay too much attention to it; they invested on faith. I raised about half the money and Edward Pressman (the executive producer) the other half. We started in July of 1972.

"The critics talked about influences on the picture and in most cases referred to films I had never seen. My influences were books like *The Hardy Boys, Swiss Family Robinson, Tom Sawyer, Huck Finn*—all involving an innocent in a drama over his or her head. I didn't actually think about those books before I did the script, but it's obvious to me now. Nancy Drew, the children's story child detective—I did think about her.

"There is some humor in the picture, I believe. Not jokes. It lies in Holly's mis-estimation of her audience, of what they will be interested in or ready to believe. (She seems at times to think of her narration as like what you get in audiovisual courses in high school.) When they're crossing the badlands, instead of telling us what's going on between Kit and herself, or anything of what we'd like and have to know, she described what they ate and what it tasted like, as though we might be planning a similar trip and appreciate her experience, this way.

"She's a typical southern girl in her desire to help, to give hard facts; not to dwell upon herself, which to her would be unseemly, but always to keep in mind the needs of others. She wants to come off in the best possible light, but she's scrupulous enough to take responsibility where in any way she might have contributed."

I suggest to Malick that the film has been criticized for patronizing Holly and her milieu. "That's foolishness. I grew up around people like Kit and Holly. I see no gulf between them and myself. One of the things the actors and I used to talk about was never stepping outside the characters and winking at the audience, never getting off the hook. If you keep your hands off the characters you open yourself to charges like that; at least you have no defense against them. What I find patronizing is people not leaving the characters alone, stacking the deck for them, not respecting their integrity, their difference.

"Holly's southerness is essential to taking her right. She isn't indifferent about her father's death, but she wouldn't think of telling you about it. It would not be proper. You should always feel there are large parts of her experience she's not including because she has a strong, if misplaced, sense of propriety. You might well wonder how anyone going through what she does could be at all concerned with proprieties. But she is. And her kind of cliché didn't begin with pulp magazines, as some critics have suggested. It exists in Nancy Drew and Tom Sawyer. It's not the mark of a diminished, pulp-fed mind, I'm trying to say, but of the 'innocent abroad.' When people express what is most important to them, it often comes out in clichés. That doesn't make them laughable; it's something tender about them. As though in struggling to reach what's more personal about them they could only come up with what's most public.

"Holly is in a way the more important character; at least you get a glimpse of what she's like. And I liked women characters better than men; they're more open to things around them, more demonstrative. Kit, on the other hand, is a closed book, not a rare trait in people who have tasted more than their share of bitterness in life. The movies have kept up a myth that suffering makes you deep. It inclines you to say deep things. It builds character and is generally healthful. It teaches you lessons you never forget. People who've suffered go around in movies with long, thoughtful faces, as though everything had caved in just yesterday. It's not that way in real life, though, not always. Suffering can make you shallow and just the opposite of vulnerable, dense. It's had this kind of effect on Kit.

"Kit doesn't see himself as anything sad or pitiable, but as a subject of incredible interest, to himself and to future generations. Like Holly, like a child, he can only really believe in what's going on inside him. Death, other people's feelings, the consequences of his actions—they're all sort of abstract for him. He thinks of himself as a successor to James Dean—a rebel without a cause—when in reality he's more like an Eisenhower conservative. 'Consider the minority opinion,' he says into the rich man's tape recorder, 'but try to get along with the majority opinion once it's accepted.' He doesn't really believe any of this, but he envies the people who do, who can. He wants to be like them, like the rich man he locks in the closet, the only man he doesn't kill, the only man he sympathizes with, and the one least in need of sympathy. It's not infrequently the people at the bottom who most vigorously defend the very rules that put and keep them there.

"And there's something about growing up in the Midwest. There's no check on you. People imagine it's the kind of place where your behavior is under constant observation, where you really have to toe the line. They got that idea from Sinclair Lewis. But people can really get ignored there and fall into bad soil. Kit did, and he grew up like a big poisonous weed.

"I don't think he's a character peculiar to his time. I tried to keep the 1950s to a bare minimum. Nostalgia is a powerful feeling; it can drown out anything. I wanted the picture to set up like a fairy tale, outside time, like *Treasure Island.* I hoped this would, among other things, take a little of the sharpness out of the violence but still keep its dreamy quality. Children's books are full of violence. Long John Silver slits the throats of the faithful crew. Kit and Holly even think of themselves as living in a fairy tale. Holly says, 'Sometimes I wish I could fall asleep and be taken off to some magical land, but this never happened.' But she enough believed there is such a place that she must confess to you she never got there."

Michel Ciment in *Positif*

Malick begins the interview with a biographical sketch.

I was born in Waco, Texas, and raised in Austin, Texas, and Oklahoma. I was named a Rhodes Scholar and received a fellowship to study at Magdalen College in Oxford, England. I didn't complete my fellowship; I left my studies in my first year and began working for the *New Yorker.* I went to Bolivia to write an article on Che Guevera's cause and the trial of Régis Debray. I spent four months there, but I didn't publish anything. Over a period of eight months, I did write other things for the *New Yorker,* including obituaries for Martin Luther King and Robert Kennedy.

I returned to the United States, where I taught philosophy at MIT for one year. In the fall of 1969, I realized I wasn't a good teacher and should leave teaching, but I didn't know what to do next. I'd always liked movies without ever being a true cinephile. When I heard that the American Film Institute had just opened and was accepting applications for their master's program, I decided to apply. Today I would certainly not be accepted, but at the time it wasn't well known, and they accepted just about anyone. I'd never made any films. At the end of my second year at the AFI, I started to work on *Badlands*.

During my studies at the AFI, I made a short film called *Lanton Mills* with some friends. It was the story of two cowboys who leave the West on horseback, enter the modern world, and try to rob a bank. I acted in it along with Warren Oates and Harry Dean Stanton, whom you might have seen in *Dillinger* and *Godfather II*. I didn't really know what I was doing, and acting in the film was a distraction. I was far from satisfied. While I was at the institute, I wrote, and above all rewrote, screenplays. I made a name for myself in rewriting. I studied in the morning, and I went to the studio in the afternoon. I worked on the first screenplay of *Dirty Harry* that Irvin Kershner was supposed to direct with Marlon Brando in the lead. Kershner and I were very excited about the film, and we worked on it together for two months. In the end, Don Siegel directed the film using a very different screenplay. I also worked on *Pocket Money* for six weeks, *Drive, He Said,* for two weeks, *Dead Head Miles,* and other projects.

How did you come up with the idea for Badlands?

I wanted to make a film about an adolescent girl. We're more open as teenagers. We ask ourselves questions that we later avoid. This is particularly true for young women in the United States, who are less inhibited than young men. In terms of actually coming up with the idea, I can't talk about it because I'm legally bound to keep it a secret.

Your film belongs to a long tradition of "lovers-on-the-lam," beginning with You Only Live Once, They Live by Night, Gun Crazy, *and* Bonnie and Clyde.

Strangely enough, I'd only seen *Bonnie and Clyde* before shooting. What interested me was how the murders compromised the young woman. Today it's hard to compromise a young woman. We're no longer living at a time like Jane Austen's when having an affair was enough to compromise a young woman. Today it takes at least a murder to get the same result: she loses her footing. I thought one of the film's ironies would be that even a series of murders would not truly compromise someone like Holly. She'd continue to have both feet on the ground; she'd be unshakable.

The story seemed powerful in and of itself to me. I knew that a big studio might be interested in the film, but I wouldn't be able to control its production. So I decided to produce an independent film. Much like a Broadway show, I produced it through a partnership agreement, which means that a lot of people contributed a small sum of money. Raising the money took a long time. In fact, it took longer to raise half of the money I needed than it took to shoot the film. The other half was raised by Ed Pressman.

We shot the film in the summer of 1972 in the southeast of Colorado, the Dust Bowl, and South Dakota for three hundred thousand dollars. Things started out well but went downhill as we ran out of money: a terrible fire destroyed some equipment and seriously injured the special-effects technician. Soon our team was made up of only four or five people. The shooting took longer than expected because we didn't have enough money. I stopped shooting to write screenplays, and that took almost a year.

The film is very similar to the original screenplay except for the scenes in the forest, which were improvised. I'd searched locations and auditioned the actors before shooting because I thought that it would be easier to raise money if I had something to show potential investors. In the end, they never wanted to see anything. We kept all of the scenes that we shot with the exception of a sequence in which Kit goes into a radio station to send a message back home.

Were you thinking about the juxtaposition of Holly's voiceover and the images on the screen from the outset?

Absolutely, but I tried to limit the voiceover in the screenplay because big distribution companies tend to dislike voiceover; they don't find it particularly cinematic. One of the reasons I didn't feel as if I could improvise, and kept to the original screenplay, had to do with all of the complications in making the film. I had to take care of everything. We were shooting at private properties without authorization: the police were looking for us along with the IRS. We, ourselves, were on the run and wanted by the authorities, and I didn't have the time or the confidence in myself to improvise. Moreover, while I was shooting my short, I believed in the myth of improvisation without realizing that in following your instincts, you can end up with the best or the worst results. However, for my next film, I hope to be freer in my shooting, less constrained by my initial ideas.

How did you deal with the problems of relating the voiceover to the images and moving between voiceover and dialogue?

It's relatively easy with the Moviola, since you can adjust the transitions as you see fit. It's obvious when a voiceover is manipulating the audience, for instance, when it communicates information that the audience should be learning through another means. But when the voiceover doesn't have a direct relationship to what's happening, as is the case in *Badlands,* it seems to work better. It also allows you to quickly solve problems that take too much time to set up and are of no real interest to today's viewers: how did they get there, how long did it take, etc.

I wanted Holly to talk like a fourteen-year-old who's trying to come off in the best possible light. It's not that she's simple-minded; she just thinks this is how she should talk when speaking to other people. She's not trying to influence the story or to promote herself, since she's careful to admit her mistakes. But her admission doesn't go much beyond regret that she threw out her fish when it was sick. Perhaps this act sets everything in motion.

The voiceover was essential. It allowed a certain humor stemming from Holly's false ideas about her audience. She has no idea what the audience will think of what she says, and she doesn't know what interests the audience. As they're crossing the badlands, she imagines we aren't interested in what's happening between Kit and herself, but rather in what they eat during the trip, how they get gas, etc., in case we go on the same trip. She doesn't really know her audience.

She actually plays a role by "acting" as a historical commentator, just as Kit plays the role of James Dean.

In both cases, acting isn't easy—it's contradictory. Kit sees himself as a rebel without a cause, and so he's very conservative; he would have been an Eisenhower conservative. When he's talking into the tape recorder at the rich man's house, he gives fatherly advice, or the advice given in a civics course. He thinks most of the people he kills are worthless. The only person he doesn't kill, and who could be a potential threat, is the rich man. But he spares him because he's a man after his own heart. He spares him, but not the friend he was working with. It's another side of his conservatism, his respect for American values.

He actually defends social order and doesn't like it when people litter. And yet, while driving his car, he becomes a rebel. He knows about nature through *National Geographic,* but he doesn't seem in tune with his own emotions, his own motivations.

Holly is like characters in *Tom Sawyer* or *Treasure Island* who, like her, adopt a way of life. But they do it naturally, without perversion. Kit thinks he's a character of incredible importance, but he can't measure his own importance. He builds a rock pile marking the place where he's arrested; he buries things in the desert; he leaves his "relics," thinking that in the future people will make money on them and come to realize his place in time. In the end, the sadness emanating from the film partially comes from the fact that Kit's most well-placed biographer, Holly, is living another life. And so his story dries up without leaving a trace.

Why doesn't Kit kill the couple who comes to visit his friend?

He shoots at them in the cellar without knowing exactly what he wants to do. He acts according to a set of rules that must be followed in such circumstances—killing all the witnesses, for instance. But he isn't sure of himself; he doesn't really know what's expected of him as a criminal. I saw Kit and Holly as young characters in *Huckleberry Finn, The Swiss Family Robinson,* and *Treasure Island*: they are lost in nature. They entertain themselves by making traps, oubliettes, and secret passageways; they invent a code; Kit gives Holly shooting lessons.

They only know how to act based on what's going on inside them. They don't communicate with the outside world. They don't understand what others feel, but it doesn't mean that they are emotionless or insensitive.

The sequences in the forest are reminiscent of Vietnam. And Kit and Holly talk about the Russian invasion and nuclear war.

In the fifties, the fear of an impending Soviet invasion was widespread in the Midwest. We were trained in civil defense against a nuclear attack. At school, we crawled under the desks. People were building shelters.

There is great violence in your film, but it's latent. You don't spend a lot of time on the sorts of violent scenes that abound in American cinema today.

I was raised in a violent environment in Texas. What struck me was how violence erupted and ended before you really had time to understand what was happening. Take, for instance, Lee Harvey Oswald's murder by Ruby: it took place in a flash. Kit and Holly—and in this respect they are truly children—don't think that death is an end. It's a "crossing to the other side." He's obsessed with his own death and wonders what the papers will say.

It must have been difficult to re-create on screen an era that is neither contemporary nor historical—it's only ten or fifteen years ago. It must have been more difficult than setting the film in the thirties or forties.

First of all, perfectly re-creating an era didn't interest me. And in this respect, having such limited means actually helped me avoid such thinking. Moreover, if you make a successful film about the past, there is no way to avoid nostalgia. So I tried keeping the references to the fifties to a bare minimum, and when they were necessary—for the music—I tried to choose tunes that were not especially of the fifties, like Nat King Cole's music. I didn't want to be too realistic, too precise, since I wanted to create a fairy-tale quality.

How did you choose the music for the film?

Irvin Kershner introduced me to the piece by Carl Orff. I'd never heard it in a film. The piece by Satie created a feeling of melancholia contrasting with the piece by Orff, which is in a major key and uplifting. Satie's music went well with the scenes where Holly's walking on the grass, when she's looking at the rich man's house, or when the plane takes them back to South Dakota at the end. Orff's music accompanies the house fire, the scenes in the forest, and the helicopter's taking off.

You introduce pauses in the forward progression of the narrative: the house in flames, shots of nature, images from the stereopticon, the newsreel.

That newsreel was in fact shot for the film! But there was no particular reason for the pauses. With the fire, I wanted to show that Holly was putting the past behind her, even if she wasn't aware of it, even if she was thinking about continuing her studies at Kit's suggestion. This once again shows Kit's conservative side.

I wasn't able to express what I wanted with the shots of animals in nature: Kit feels for the animals living alone on the prairie who are left to their own devices. The lab lost a part of our negative that had one of my favorite shots, an image of water birds taking flight, which symbolized Kit's desire to leave, to go elsewhere and start a new life. He feels closer to the animals than he does to the rich man, or even to Holly, who for him is more like a sounding board who's ten years younger than he is. No woman his age would tolerate him or take part in his fantasy world.

On the other hand, I do like the sequence with the stereopticon in which Holly thinks her life could have taken another course. But in the same sequence she doesn't seem sad that it hasn't. She accepts her fate in life. And my favorite quote from the film comes when Kit is fishing in the river, indifferent to the beauty of nature, and she says: "Sometimes I wished I could fall asleep and be taken off to some magical land." She's careful to point out, as if it were necessary to do so, "but this never happened," which shows us once again that she does not understand her audience. This should make us sympathize with her more.

I don't think that the film is cold; there's a certain warmth to it. I was very worried that people might say the film is soulless, because I admire [Elia] Kazan, [George] Stevens, and [Arthur] Penn, and scenes of great emotion. But to openly express your emotions, you have to have great maturity, which is something that my characters don't have. People believe that when you've suffered in life, you act like a wounded animal, showing your wounds as if they were fresh from the day before. And that is often what happens in films. But in real life, you hide your suffering;

it's the only way to survive. That's what happens to Kit. Far from having made them mature, deeper, and sympathetic—a myth Americans believe in—suffering has made them trite, narrow-minded, and dense. That is why Kit has become narcissistic, not in the sense that he's looking for the root cause of his problems, but rather because he's an imposter who doesn't like who he is.

Your cinematic style is very classical, very taut. To what extent did you work with your cameramen?

I had three cameramen, but I had problems with the first two and really only worked closely with the last one, Steven Larner, who studied at the IDHEC [Institut des Hautes Etudes Cinematographiques] and was Ghislain Cloquet's assistant. He was my professor at the AFI. He shot the best scenes of the film—the fire, most of the chase, and most of the sequences at night. He's truly remarkable, and it's too bad he isn't used more often. He has a luminous style. He had previously worked on *Lion's Love.*

I didn't want to use filters. Many people find that the Eastmancolor negative is too saturated, and so they use techniques—filters, lighting, screens—that reduce saturation like [Vilmos] Zsigmond's or [László] Kovács's "flashage." The landscapes in *Badlands* are actually unsaturated, even a little grainy. I overexposed the negative and then printed it with very low contrast, so that even in exterior shots with natural light the characters never need to be lighted by reflectors.

I wanted to remain at a distance from my characters, which is why I refused to film with a handheld camera. In a fairy tale, you shouldn't interfere with a story that follows its own logic. I hope that the voiceover and the cinematography create some distance without alienating the viewer too much. They should distance you, and then make you participate, then distance you again, in a back-and-forth movement.

I was worried that the audience would patronize the characters if they became too involved. If you feel that you understand them perfectly, you have no respect for them in the end; you reject them. I didn't want their lives to end with the end of the film. I wanted them to live beyond the end of the film with the sort of autonomy that people we encounter, but never befriend, have. This is particularly true for Kit.

How did you choose Sissy Spacek and Martin Sheen?

She had acted before in Michael Richie's *Prime Cut*. She embodies the character, and she comes from Texas like me. I ended up having the character come from Texas instead of South Dakota, as I had originally written the roles. Sissy and I come from the same area and have had similar experiences.

I found Martin Sheen by chance, even though he had acted before. He didn't want to act in an independent film because they're always so precarious. But in the end he worked even between takes, because as our money diminished, so did our technical team. He worked with me on his character's dialogue. He was a little too old for the role—about thirty years old—but I chose him because he wasn't like actors who come from rich families in New York or California. For them, their parents' money allows them to wait around until they find a role. Even if they are broke, they are still well-off because they can always count on their families. But Martin comes from a working-class family. He has nine brothers and a sister. His real name is Ramon Estevez (his first name comes from Ramon Novarro); his father was a doorman at a bank in Dayton, Ohio. On weekdays, the kids worked at a factory, and on Sunday, they were caddies at a golf club. The other actors didn't have the authenticity he could bring to the role. I didn't know his life story in detail, but there was no mistaking that he had something genuine about him.

A complete, updated list of Terrence Malick's work in film, credited and uncredited, can be found at the Internet Movie Database (http://imdb.com).

Badlands (1973, USA)
Director: Terrence Malick
Screenplay: Terrence Malick
Production Company: Pressman-Williams Enterprises
Executive Producer: Edward Pressman
Producer: Terrence Malick
Cinematography: Brian Probyn, Tak Fujimoto, Stevan Larner
Editor: Robert Estrin
Associate Editor: William Weber
Art Directors: Jack Fisk, Ed Richardson
Music: George Tipton
Sound Editor: James Nelson
Length: 95 minutes
Lead Cast: Martin Sheen (Kit Carruthers), Sissy Spacek (Holly), Warren
    Oates (Father), Ramon Bieri (Cato)

Days of Heaven (1978, USA)
Director: Terrence Malick
Screenplay: Terrence Malick
Production Company: O. P. Productions, Paramount Pictures Corporation
Executive Producer: Jacob Brackman
Producers: Bert Schneider, Harold Schneider
Cinematography: Nestor Almendros
Additional Cinematography: Haskell Wexler
Editor: Billy Weber
Art Director: Jack Fisk
Music: Ennio Morricone
Length: 95 minutes

Lead Cast: Richard Gere (Bill), Brooke Adams (Abby), Sam Shepard (The Farmer), Linda Manz (Linda), Robert Wilke (Farm Foreman)

The Thin Red Line (1998, Canada/USA)
Director: Terrence Malick
Screenplay: Terrence Malick
Production Company: Twentieth Century Fox, Fox 2000 Pictures, Phoenix Pictures
Executive Producer: George Stevens Jr.
Producers: Robert Michael Geisler, John Roberdeau, Grant Hill
Based on novel by: James Jones
Cinematography: John Toll
Editors: Billy Weber, Leslie Jones, Saar Klein
Production Designer: Jack Fisk
Art Director: Ian Gracie
Music: Hans Zimmer
Length: 170 minutes
Lead Cast: Sean Penn (First Sergeant Welsh), Adrien Brody (Corporal Fife), James Caviezel (Private Witt), Ben Chaplin (Private Bell), George Clooney (Captain Bosche), John Cusack (Captain Gaff), Woody Harrelson (Sergeant Keck), Elias Koteas (Captain Staros), Nick Nolte (Lieutenant Colonel Tall), John C. Reilly (Sergeant Storm), John Savage (Sergeant McCron), Paul Gleeson (First Lieutenant Band), Arie Verveen (Private Dale), Dash Mihok (Private Doll), John Travolta (Brigadier General Quintard), Jared Leto (Second Lieutenant Whyte)

The New World (2005, USA)
Director: Terrence Malick
Screenplay: Terrence Malick
Production Company: Sarah Green Productions for New Line Cinema
Producer: Sarah Green
Cinematography: Emmanuel Lubezki
Editors: Richard Chew, Hank Corwin, Saar Klein, Mark Yoshikawa
Production Designer: Jack Fisk
Art Director: David Crank
Music: James Horner
Length: 135 minutes
Lead Cast: Colin Farrell (Captain Smith), Q'orianka Kilcher (Pocahontas), Christopher Plummer (Captain Newport), Christian Bale (John Rolfe), August Schellenberg (Powhatan), Wes Studi (Opechancanough), David Thewlis (Wingfield)

Almendros, Nestor. *Man with a Camera.* Trans. Rachel Phillips Belash. New York: Farrar, Straus, and Giroux, 1984.

Bersani, Leo, and Ulysse Dutoit. *Forms of Being: Cinema, Aesthetics, Subjectivity.* London: British Film Institute, 2004.

Bignell, Jonathan. "From Detail to Meaning: *Badlands* (Terrence Malick, 1973) and Cinematic Articulation." In *Style and Meaning: Studies in the Detailed Analysis of Film.* Ed. John Gibbs and Douglas Pye. Manchester, Eng.: Manchester University Press, 2005. 42–52.

Biskind, Peter. *Easy Riders, Raging Bulls: How the Sex-Drugs–and Rock 'n' Roll Generation Saved Hollywood.* London: Bloomsbury, 1998.

———. "The Runaway Genius." *Vanity Fair* 460 (December 1998): 202–20.

Cain, Jimmie. "'Writing in His Musical Key': Terrence Malick's Vision of *The Thin Red Line.*" *Film Criticism* 25.1 (2000): 2–24.

Carter, Rusty. "'New World' Is Mixed." *Virginia Gazette,* December 10, 2005.

Cavell, Stanley. *The World Viewed.* Enlarged ed. Cambridge, Mass.: Harvard University Press, 1979.

Chion, Michel. *The Thin Red Line.* Trans. Trista Selous. London: British Film Institute, 2004.

Corrigan, Timothy. *A Cinema without Walls: Movies and Culture after Vietnam.* New Brunswick, N.J.: Rutgers University Press, 1991.

Critchley, Simon. "Calm—On Terrence Malick's *The Thin Red Line.*" *Film-Philosophy* 6.38 (December 2002). http://www.film-philosophy.com/vol6–2002/n48critchley.

Denerstein, Robert. "Malick Underdoes It in Plodding 'New World.'" *Rocky Mountain News,* January 20, 2006. http://www.rockymountainnews.com/drmn/movies/article/0,2792,DRMN_23_4400094,00.html.

Dixon, Wheeler Winston. *Visions of Paradise: Images of Eden in the Cinema.* New Brunswick, N.J.: Rutgers University Press, 2006.

Doherty, Thomas. Rev. of *The Thin Red Line,* dir. Terrence Malick. *Cineaste* 24.2–3 (Spring/Summer 1999): 83–84.

Donougho, Martin. "West of Eden: Terrence Malick's *Days of Heaven.*" *Post Script* 5.1 (Fall 1984): 17–30.

Ebert, Roger. "Days of Heaven." *Chicago Sun-Times,* December 7, 1997. http://rogerebert.suntimes.com/apps/pbcs.dll/article?AID=/19971207/REVIEWS08/401010327/1023.

Flanagan, Martin. "'Everything a Lie': The Critical and Commercial Reception of Terrence Malick's *The Thin Red Line.*" In *The Cinema of Terrence Malick: Poetic Visions of America.* Ed. Hannah Patterson. London: Wallflower, 2003. 123–36.

Heidegger, Martin. *The Essence of Reasons.* Trans. Terrence Malick. Evanston, Ill.: Northwestern University Press, 1969.

Henderson, Brian. "Exploring *Badlands.*" *Wide Angle* 5.4 (1983): 38–51.

Hoberman, J. "Mr. and Mrs. Smith." Rev. of *The New World,* dir. Terrence Malick. *Village Voice,* December 27, 2005, 56.

———. "The Wars Within." Rev. of *The Thin Red Line,* dir. Terrence Malick. *Village Voice,* December 29, 1998, 117.

Hodgkins, John. "In the Wake of Desert Storm: A Consideration of Modern World War II Films." *Journal of Popular Film and Television* 30.2 (Summer 2002): 74–84.

Jones, James. *The Thin Red Line.* 1962; reprint, New York: Delta, 1998.

Jones, Kent. "Acts of God." *Film Comment* 242 (March/April 2006): 24–26, 28.

Kael, Pauline. *When the Lights Go Down.* New York: Holt, Rinehart, and Winston, 1980.

Karten, Harvey S. Rev. of *The New World,* dir. Terrence Malick. *Arizona Reporter,* December 22, 2005.

Keathley, Christian. *Cinephilia and History; or, the Wind in the Trees.* Bloomington: Indiana University Press, 2005.

Kinder, Marsha. "The Return of the Outlaw Couple." *Film Quarterly* 27.4 (Summer 1974): 2–10.

Lee, Hwanhee. "Terrence Malick." *Senses of Cinema.* http://www.sensesofcinema.com/contents/directors/02/malick.html (accessed May 9, 2007).

Lewis, R. W. B. *The American Adam: Innocence, Tragedy, and Tradition in the Nineteenth Century.* Chicago: University of Chicago Press, 1954.

Major, Wade. Rev. of *The New World,* dir. Terrence Malick. *Box Office Online Reviews.* http://www.boxoffice.com/scripts/fiw.dll?GetReview?&where=ID&terms=8487 (accessed December 22, 2005).

Martin, Adrian. "Things to Look Into: The Cinema of Terrence Malick." *Rouge.* http://rouge.com.au/10/malick.html (accessed March 30, 2008).

Marx, Leo. *The Machine in the Garden.* New York: Oxford University Press, 1964.

Mast, Gerald, and Bruce F. Kawin. *A Short History of the Movies.* 9th ed. New York: Pearson, 2007.

McCabe, Colin. "Bayonets in Paradise." *Sight and Sound* 9.2 (February 1999): 11–14.

McCann, Ben. "'Enjoying the Scenery': Landscape and the Fetishisation of Nature in *Badlands* and *Days of Heaven*." In *The Cinema of Terrence Malick: Poetic Visions of America*. Ed. Hannah Patterson. London: Wallflower, 2003. 75–85.

McGettigan, Joan. "*Days of Heaven* and the Myth of the West." In *The Cinema of Terrence Malick: Poetic Visions of America*. Ed. Hannah Patterson. London: Wallflower, 2003. 50–60.

————. "Interpreting a Man's World: Female Voices in *Badlands* and *Days of Heaven*." *Journal of Film and Video* 52.4 (2001): 33–43.

Melville, Herman. *Moby Dick*. New York: Norton, 1967.

Michaels, Lloyd. *The Phantom of the Cinema: Character in Modern Film*. Albany: State University of New York Press, 1998.

Morrison, James. Rev. of *The Thin Red Line,* dir. Terrence Malick. *Film Quarterly* 53.1 (1999): 35–38.

Morrison, James, and Thomas Schur. *The Films of Terrence Malick*. Westport: Praeger, 2003.

Mottram, Ron. "All Things Shining: The Struggle for Wholeness, Redemption, and Transcendence in the Films of Terrence Malick." In *The Cinema of Terrence Malick: Poetic Visions of America*. Ed. Hannah Patterson. London: Wallflower, 2003. 13–23.

Orr, John. "A Cinema of Poetry." In *Post-War Cinema and Modernity*. Ed. John Orr and Olga Taxidou. New York: New York University Press, 2001. 133–44.

————. "Terrence Malick and Arthur Penn: The Western Re-Myth." In *The Cinema of Terrence Malick: Poetic Visions of America*. Ed. Hannah Patterson. London: Wallflower, 2003. 61–74.

Petrakis, John. "American Beginnings." *Christian Century* 123.1 (January 10, 2006): 49.

Petric, Vlada. "Days of Heaven." *Film Quarterly* 32.2 (Winter 1978–79): 37–45.

Pizzello, Stephen. "The War Within." Interview with John Toll. *American Cinematographer* 80.2 (February 1999): 42–58.

Power, Richard. "Listening to the Aquarium: The Symbolic Use of Music in *Days of Heaven*." In *The Cinema of Terrence Malick: Poetic Visions of America*. Ed. Hannah Patterson. London: Wallflower, 2003. 100–109.

Rainer, Peter. "'World' Turns Slowly (but It Sure Is Pretty)." Rev. of *The New World,* dir. Terrence Malick. *Christian Science Monitor,* January 20, 2006, 11.

Rothman, William, and Marian Keane. *Reading Cavell's* The World Viewed: *A Philosophical Perspective on Film*. Detroit: Wayne State University Press, 2000.

Schaffer, Bill. "The Shape of Fear: Thoughts after *The Thin Red Line*." *Senses of Cinema*. http://www.sensesofcinema.com/contents/00/8/thinredline.html (accessed March 30, 2008).

Schonberg, Harold C. "Days of Heaven." *New York Times*, September 14, 1978, 96.

Shepard, Jim. "*Badlands* and the 'Innocence' of American Innocence." *The Believer* 1.1 (March 2003): 39–47.

Silberman, Robert. "Terrence Malick, Landscape, and 'This War at the Heart of Nature.'" In *The Cinema of Terrence Malick: Poetic Visions of America*. Ed. Hannah Patterson. London: Wallflower, 2003. 160–72.

Sterritt, David. "Film, Philosophy, and Terrence Malick's 'The New World.'" *Chronicle of Higher Education* 52.18 (January 6, 2006): B12–13.

Streamas, John. "The Greatest Generation Steps over *The Thin Red Line*." In *The Cinema of Terrence Malick: Poetic Visions of America*. Ed. Hannah Patterson. London: Wallflower, 2003. 137–47.

Swafford, Jan. *Charles Ives: A Life with Music*. New York: Norton, 1996.

Taylor, Charles. "The Big Dead One." Rev. of *The Thin Red Line*, dir. Terrence Malick. *Salon*. http://www.salon.com/ent/movies/reviews/1999/01/cov_08reviewa.html (accessed March 30, 2008).

Thompson, Anne. "Risky Business: Will Silence Be Golden for Spielberg, Malick?" *Hollywood Reporter*, December 2, 2005.

Thomson, David. *The New Biographical Dictionary of Film*. New York: Knopf, 2004.

Walker, Beverly. "Malick on *Badlands*." *Sight and Sound* 44.2 (Spring 1975): 82–83.

Whalen, Tom. "'Maybe All Men Got One Big Soul': The Hoax within the Metaphysics of Terrence Malick's *The Thin Red Line*." *Literature/Film Quarterly* 27.3 (1999): 162–66.

Wondra, Janet. "Marx in a Texas Love Triangle: 'Marrying Up' and the Classed Gaze in *Days of Heaven*." *Journal of Film and Video* 57.4 (Winter 2005): 3–18.

Zacharek, Stephanie. Rev. of *The New World*, dir. Terrence Malick. *Salon*. http://dir.salon.com/story/ent/movies/review/2005/12/23/new_world/index.html (accessed March 30, 2008).

Zaller, Robert. "Raising the Seventies: The Early Films of Terrence Malick." *Boulevard* 15.1–2 (1999): 141–55.

Zucker, Carole. "'God Don't Even Hear You,' or Paradise Lost: Terrence Malick's *Days of Heaven*." *Literature/Film Quarterly* 29.1 (2001): 2–9.

New Line Cinema, 19
New World, The (2005), 2–4, 19, 55, 78–98
Nolan, Christopher, 81
Nolte, Nick, 3, 58, 62
Nostalgia, 36, 105, 110
Nuclear war, 110

Oates, Warren, 15, 27, 106
O'Connor, Flannery, 15
Orff, Carl, 33, 110–11
Orr, John, 21
Oswald, Lee Harvey, 110
Ozu, Yasujiro, 6, 84–85

Pacino, Al, 39
Paradise. *See* Eden
Paramount Pictures Corporation, 17–18
Parker, Bonnie, 6
Pasolini, Pier Paolo, 28
Passion of the Christ, The (2004), 68
"Peaceable Kingdom, The," 27
Penn, Arthur, 2, 6, 21–22, 23–24, 111
Penn, Sean, 58, 62
Percy, Walker, 57
Petric, Vlada, 40, 82
Philosophy in Malick's films, 4–5, 12, 39, 61–62, 74, 75, 95
Platoon (1986), 63, 65
Pocahontas (1995), 79
Pocket Money (1972), 15, 102, 106
Postmodernism, 4, 7
Power, Richard, 53
Pressman, Edward, 103, 107
Psychological explanations, Malick's avoidance of. *See* Characterization in Malick's films
Pullman, Bill, 57–58
Pynchon, Thomas, 1

Rafelson, Bob, 2
Railroad. *See* Trains
Rainer, Peter, 84, 85
Rambo, First Blood (1982), 65
Redemption, personal, 8, 88, 89, 91. *See also* Transcendence, personal
Redford, Robert, 19

Religion in Malick's films, 74, 81, 88–89, 91–92
Resnais, Alain, 24
Riva, Emmanuelle, 24
Roberdeau, John, 57, 58
Rohmer, Eric, 6, 84–85
Role playing. *See under* Characterization in Malick's films
Romanticism in Malick's films, 4–5, 8–9, 68, 81, 95
Romeo and Juliet, 92
Rosenberg, Stuart, 15
Rourke, Mickey, 57–58
Rousseau, Jean-Jacques, 86

Saint-Saëns, Camille, 52, 53, 80–81
Salinger, J. D., 13–14
Sanshô the Bailiff, 57
Sarris, Andrew, 40
Satie, Erik, 37, 80, 110–11
"savages," 86, 87
Saving Private Ryan (1998), 18, 58, 59, 60, 61, 63, 65
Schneider, Bert and Harold, 39
Schonberg, Harold, 40
Schur, Thomas, 5, 15, 40
Scorsese, Martin, 2
Self-reflexivity, 13, 27, 32–33, 51, 54, 73
Separation anxiety, 78
Sheen, Martin, 3, 57, 113
Shepard, Jim, 35
Shepard, Sam, 48
Signs of Life (1968), 6
Sony Pictures Classics, 57, 81
Spacek, Sissy, 7–8, 113
Spielberg, Steven, 2, 18, 23, 40, 58–60
Stanton, Harry Dean, 15, 106
Starkweather, Charles, 6, 20
Star Wars (1977), 40, 57
Steinbeck, John, 4, 45
Sterritt, David, 79
Stevens, George, 31, 111
Stevens, George, Jr., 57
Stone, Oliver, 6, 63
Straw Dogs (1971), 56
Sugarland Express, The (1974), 23
Swiss Family Robinson, The, 25, 103, 109

Lloyd Michaels is a professor in the English Department at Allegheny College. He is the author of *Elia Kazan: A Guide to References and Resources, The Phantom of the Cinema: Character in Modern Film,* and *Ingmar Bergman's Persona.* He has edited the journal *Film Criticism* since 1977.

Books in the series Contemporary Film Directors

Nelson Pereira dos Santos
    Darlene J. Sadlier

Abbas Kiarostami
    Mehrnaz Saeed-Vafa and Jonathan
    Rosenbaum

Joel and Ethan Coen
    R. Barton Palmer

Claire Denis
    Judith Mayne

Wong Kar-wai
    Peter Brunette

Edward Yang
    John Anderson

Pedro Almodóvar
    Marvin D'Lugo

Chris Marker
    Nora Alter

Abel Ferrara
    Nicole Brenez, translated by
    Adrian Martin

Jane Campion
    Kathleen McHugh

Jim Jarmusch
    Juan Suárez

Roman Polanski
    James Morrison

Manoel de Oliveira
    John Randal Johnson

Neil Jordan
    Maria Pramaggiore

Paul Schrader
    George Kouvaros

Jean-Pierre Jeunet
    Elizabeth Ezra

Terrence Malick
    Lloyd Michaels

Sally Potter
    Catherine Fowler

The University of Illinois Press
is a founding member of the
Association of American University Presses.

Composed in 10/13 New Caledonia
with Helvetica Neue display
by Celia Shapland
at the University of Illinois Press
Manufactured by Cushing-Malloy, Inc.

University of Illinois Press
1325 South Oak Street
Champaign, IL 61820-6903
www.press.uillinois.edu